"Don't Tell Mommy"

*A True Story and Memoirs of
a Child Tortured and Sexually Abused
for 12 years and Now Seeking Justice*

Mary Justice Avalon

Pay It Forward Publishing

The opinions expressed in this manuscript are solely the opinions of the author and do not represent the opinions or thoughts of the publisher. The author has represented and warranted full ownership and/or legal right to publish all the materials in this book.

"Don't Tell Mommy"
A True Story and Memoirs of a Child Tortured and Sexually Abused for 12 years and Now Seeking Justice
All Rights Reserved.
Copyright © 2014 Mary Justice Avalon
v2.0

Cover Photo © 2014 thinkstockphotos.com. All rights reserved - used with permission.

This book may not be reproduced, transmitted, or stored in whole or in part by any means, including graphic, electronic, or mechanical without the express written consent of the publisher except in the case of brief quotations embodied in critical articles and reviews.

Pay It Forward Publishing

ISBN: 978-0-578-14881-6

PRINTED IN THE UNITED STATES OF AMERICA

I am dedicating this book to my beautiful, intelligent children who may not have had a perfect childhood, but I made sure it was nothing like mine. I am so proud of the young adults they have both become. I believe they now understand choices I have made in my life and I hope they forever choose happiness over everything because that is what is truly important at the end of the day. Hopefully they will never read this book, or not until I have passed on from this earth. As their mother, I do not want them to know me as I once was…weak, helpless, and a long time victim who struggled with incredible fears throughout all my childhood and unfortunately into my adult years. It's a tough situation I am risking putting myself in. But I'll never "rest easy" until the burden is lifted. They understand. I am blessed with wonderful children and I pray God blesses them for the rest of their lives; I am honored to be their mother.

I also would like to dedicate this experience now on paper to my husband of 5 years+ now, whom I truly adore and respect. He has had to deal with some erratic behavior on my part due to the damage my stepfather has caused me, emotionally and physically. He is patient and has taught me what true love is and accepts me for who I am, damaged, broken, but optimistic and having faith in fate. Each day is a new day in a better life. He has allowed me to take time to tell my story knowing the process would not be easy emotionally or financially. He is an incredible man. I am grateful to have him as my husband.

I would also like to thank my mother. I had to ask her difficult questions and admire her honesty and willingness to help bring this story public because she knew how much it would help me heal and move on. I am sorry to cause any unpleasant situations and memories to my family that may result in the publication and publicity of this book, but it is necessary and long overdue.

I hope the privacy of my family will be protected and respected. This is an ugly tale and the premise for it is to be able to have closure, express my emotions in a manner to help others who have had to deal with any form that may be related to any horrifying situation, and also hopefully protect any future victims that may fall in my former stepfather's predatorily path.

I have found that having the people you love that truly care about you in your life gives you the strength to do anything…this is my anything.

Contents

Summary vii

Important Notes from the Author viii

A Personal Note To My Former Stepfather… x

Introduction xi

Chapter 1   Marrying for Love or Did He Hit the Jackpot? 1

Chapter 2   Cupcake 4

Chapter 3   The "Boogey Man" is Real 8

Chapter 4   Scared Shitless and Living a Freakin' Nightmare 12

chapter 5   Never Judge a Book by Its Cover 14

chapter 6   Dear Lord, Where are you? 16

Chapter 7   School Became My New Savior 22

Chapter 8   Silence Isn't Always Golden 24

Chapter 9   Honor Thy Sister? 27

Chapter 10   Dirty Deeds 34

Chapter 11   My Saving Graces ☺ 54

Chapter 12   Will It Ever End? 60

Chapter 13   Don't Mess With Mother Nature?   I'll take My Chances…   Crap…I'm Evolving! 66

Chapter 14 Meet The Fellas… 68

Chapter 15 Hubba Hubba! 70

Chapter 16 My Own Endless Love 82

Chapter 17 Can I Pull Of Being *Normal*? 87

Chapter 18 Best Day…Worst Day Ever 90

Chapter 19 Dumb Blonde...101

Chapter 20 I Grew a Pair?..105

Chapter 21 Sweet Dreams Are Made of *This*…Asshole! 109

Chapter 22 My First? ☺ 119

Chapter 23 The Apple Doesn't Fall Far From the Tree, Does It?...123

Chapter 24 It's All in the Family 126

Chapter 25 Oh Boy?!? 128

Chapter 26 But Wait…There's More..130

Chapter 27 So Many Women, Where in Hell Did He
 Find the Time?..133

Chapter 28 Sick or Serial?..134

Chapter 29 Time to Pay the Piper 137

Chapter 30 I Didn't Make *Justice* Part of my Pseudo Name
 for Nothing!..138

Worth mentioning…...141

Summary

A woman who is now in her late 40's finally tells her story of horrifying secrets of growing up in the Poconos with an incestuous stepfather who she could never punish for the unthinkable crimes he committed against her and her family. She hopes to seek her own form of divine justice, and closure with this reality finally displayed on paper and someday hopefully on the big screen. The main premise for this book is for this monster who stole her childhood to realize it's all about **"him"**.

*It is graphic and the author holds nothing back and this is because she feels it is necessary for people know what some pedophiles are doing to children and hopes to raise awareness to the growing epidemic of victims too afraid to speak out on their abusers. No one should *ever* be afraid to tell.

Important Notes from the Author...

Due to the sensitive nature of the topic and in depth details, all names of these actual people and actual places where this true story has taken place have been altered to protect the privacy of others who also have fallen victim to this sick individual. I myself am using a fictitious name to remain anonymous for the safety of myself and my family because **he is still out there**. I encourage those who realize who this sick individual is and may have had fallen victim to him to come forward and not be afraid to speak out against him. My statute of limitations expired when I turned 30 long ago. Now I can't stop him alone, not legally anyway. I pray for him to seek help and turn himself in. Do the right thing...after all these years...it's time he should face up to what he has done to me and countless others.

I would also like parents to be advised **this book should not be in the hands of their young loved ones due to the extreme sexual graphic content and language. Use discretion in discussions with young individuals. Anyone may be at risk of the heinous crime of molestation or sexual child abuse of any kind, incest included. But definitely talk to your children! Become familiar with those who have access to your children. It may give them the courage to tell Mommy...tell someone...tell anyone who can help them avoid extreme situations!** This book will help you know some signs to look for and hopefully give parents courage to discuss this typically taboo topic and communicate better with their children on the subject. But the bottom line is that it is **our** job as parents to **ASK** the questions, no matter what or about whom. Open communication with our kids is critical!

*Know this...only I, my stepfather, and his other victims know what *"he"* did...and now those close to him hopefully will know too.

IMPORTANT NOTES FROM THE AUTHOR...

People will figure it out, I'm counting on it. I don't wish him physical harm at this point in my life, but I pray he would finally (<u>*even after 42 years*</u>) take responsibility for crimes he's committed for sooooo many years to myself and God only knows how many others. He needs to pay for the mental and physical destruction he's caused to his victims.

*I want him to know I did tell Mommy <u>and finally</u>...
everyone else who will read this book.*

A Personal Note To My Former Stepfather...

Guess what "daddy"???...karma's a bitch, mother fucker. I won't be silenced any longer and now you should be the one who is afraid.

Introduction

I never thought of myself as interesting but I have an extraordinary story to tell that is long overdue and as a grown woman, I need some form of closure in order to be complete in living the rest of my life without this huge burden that has plagued me all my life. **What you're about to read is unfortunately a graphically true story about a child that lived a life of terror and constant fear for nearly twelve years with a real life "Boogey Man", her stepfather.** If nothing else I'd like this real life horror story to help parents look at their children more closely, differently, eye to eye, just in case the unimaginable is a reality for their family. I have become a "tell it like it is" type of person probably because it's true that "what doesn't kill you makes you stronger", and let's face it, I need to believe in something. I have always tried to rationalize *"why me"???*...and much more. The disgusting act of incest will never be obsolete because there will always be sick, twisted fucks who have no control over the urges to destroy the innocence of children. Some who may have been identified and faced the law may be treated for their disease; others go unrecognized and left to prey on unsuspecting victims.

> *In my eyes there will always be a "Boogey Man". My question is...will we ever see him coming and can we stop him???*

*You will find I crack little jokes and poke fun here and there with comments that may seem inappropriate to some readers. Please understand I am by NO means downplaying the seriousness of the mind blowing acts that took place, especially when the subject is that of a child. Please remember and understand this is my way of telling my story which is *extremely* emotionally for me. I try to keep my sanity and deal with making something soooo personal public in this way. I want the facts in the reading for you to be intriguing, informational, emotional, well written and so interesting that you won't want to put it down. My story needs to be heard when I have felt all my life there was no one who could listen or ever understand. I will only speak the truth to the best of my recollections. A lot went on in twelve years. I am not searching for sympathy by any means but some form of justice like knowing someday ***"he"*** will have to meet his maker for what he did to me at the very least. I find comfort in knowing he will burn in hell.

*As my story goes on, understand there are things I remember at a very young age, and then there are things I totally blacked out of my memory supposedly I guess because of the harshness of the acts. None of it is pleasant at this point and the detailed graphic sins committed on children are about to be told. I apologize to the readers in advance for the intense content but *I NEED* to tell it as it was and there is no reason to "sugar coat" the filthy dirty deeds of a sick bastard who needs to be stopped.

These people do exist and people need to know the reality of what they are capable of making innocent children do. I have heard many admit they were "molested, sexually abused, etc." I have never read explicit details that anyone has ever really told on paper in of what exactly happened to them when these acts took place. This does not mean these stories are not out there, I'm sure they are and I feel for them as well knowing now how difficult it is to see it on paper...recall every detail possible...in hopes of something good to come out of it all.

My story is different because I hope to turn the tables on my stepfather, make him live in fear of his identity being made public and pressure him into giving up his present day freedoms and finally pay justice to his victims by admitting his crimes. Too much time has passed now for me to prosecute him in the state of Pennsylvania,

INTRODUCTION

but it is never too late for the TRUTH *anywhere*…**this is America.** I was refused crucial support as a teen when I wanted to finally tell my mother and seek justice. What happens to him from this point on is not up to me. I feel now it is left up to fate and God. And I now feel God will finally take care of *this* child, the one who had always begged for answers as a young victim and lived in constant fear. I feel it's necessary to plant a seed in a parent's mind to pay more attention to their children and hopefully prevent any severe sexually inappropriate damage to their kids, no matter what their age. The freaks are always out there, *everywhere*.

…"**I was meant to tell this story**…

My dreams and nightmares for decades have told me so."

"Mary J. Avalon"

CHAPTER 1

Marrying for Love or Did He Hit the Jackpot?

IT WAS JULY 1969 when my mother who we'll refer to as Mindy, age 25, had a boyfriend only 19, we will call him Jared. He was from out of town but would travel to Bethlehem, Pennsylvania from the Poconos to see her and her three adorable blonde haired, blue eyed and very young children .Our family was made up of my older sister who we'll refer to as Maureen and was 6 years old at the time off marriage taken place, I, who will be named Katelyn, was 4 and my little brother who we will refer to as Todd, was only 2 years old.

Despite the disapproval of her boyfriend's parents to get married after only 6 months of dating (and only being 19 and didn't have a pot to piss in) Jared still insisted they marry and all move to his family's property in the "boonies" up to the Pocono Mountains of Pennsylvania. Upon only recently finding out about the disapproving attitude my "step grandparents" expressed when I was researching details with my mother about things beyond my knowledge...these facts made me realize there was a possible *"agenda"* on Jared's part right from the words he spoke "I DO"??? I do believe he hit the *jackpot*. Did he conspire to what fate was to become of these innocent children, as Mindy was just thankful a man so wonderful would even take on the responsibility of a wife and **her** three children??? He didn't have money. He didn't have any material possessions he could call his own. He was a handy man of sorts and tinkered around with cars, home repairs, plumbing, etc. He was also big on hunting...and his hunt for what he truly yearned for... was that now over? As time goes on you will learn more about his tactics related to him utilizing instruments and places around him and his unconventional usage of these things and spoken places as well as his intentions to manipulate and haunt children.

So in January of 1970 in a little white church up the hill from "the house" Jared and Mindy were wed with a small gathering of family and friends.

It started out as a multi family house which was creepy as hell at the very first glance. A two story, one hundred year old farmhouse that sort of "stared" at you with the placement of the windows...like that of the famous Amityville house, only not curved windows and it was unpainted and still looked grey and creepy like something the Adams Family lived in or The Bates Motel from the exterior. It had three fairly small bedrooms and only one bath, and I mean only one bath tub... no shower. There was a dumpy matching "outhouse" out back that had the stereotypical little crescent moon carved in the door...like that was even an option for use...(hell no, at least not for me!) I found it to be very disturbing. It looked like a place one may get locked in as a form of scary isolating punishment. This spooky house also had a big oil heating "stove" with big round "stovepipes" as I called them. These pipes ran up from the stove and through the ceiling to the upper floor. It was the main heat source. The structure contained a narrow stairwell with fourteen wooden creaky steep steps that led to the bathroom and a hall with a wooden banister. This hall then led to two bedrooms along one side of the house, and across the opposite end of that hallway you find the attic door and the biggest bedroom of the three. Plaster walls that were always in need of repair were pretty much everywhere making the house appear in need of repairs at all times. And trust me when I say there was nothing "modern" in this place whatsoever. This was in the seventies keep in mind, but the northern redneck inhabitants still managed with old yee haw artifacts that if they functioned, they used it. There was an actual cranking washing machine that you had to roll clothing through to ring out the water it was just supposedly washed and cleaned in. The house was hazardous for many reasons including crap electrical wiring. The house had only pull chain light fixtures that were just light bulbs dangling' overhead in various rooms. And three, yes *three* families would now share this redneck paradise on property in the boonies of the Poconos that would eventually become a compound of Jared's relatives. Oh, and I have to mention that there was the scariest basement and attic you would **ever** see in any horror flick. The house did NOT *"feel right"* from the start. I was young, but I knew I hated it. I never felt I could call it home. I never wanted to call it home. I never did call it home. This was the unfortunate place I HAD to grow up in. You will find that this was a place even as a young child I felt was a "bad" place and no joy would ever be remembered by me, that child, in that place. Welcome to the seriously disturbing redneck part of the Poconos. This is where my nightmare begins.

CHAPTER 2

Cupcake

TO THIS DAY I'll never forget the first encounter I had as an incest victim. Of course I didn't know that at the time and how my life would change forever. It was fall in the Poconos. Usually you would think, "Wow, what a beautiful, peaceful place to see the foliage, the beautiful mountains and endless winding country roads." Who could possibly even imagine that these gorgeous postcard settings would hold horrifying secrets? On a night that normally would be described as something quite ordinary for a typical American family was quite the opposite. Nothing would ever seem so typical or ordinary, sweet or beautiful…nothing good will ever happen in this place for me, ever. I had recently just turned six years old and it was my mother's regular Bingo night and I believe where she played was not far from the house. I believe it was a Wednesday. She fed me dinner, macaroni and cheese from a box, kissed me goodbye and said be sure to go to bed when "Daddy" tells you. As far as I can remember my brother, sister and I always called him "Daddy", even though he never legally adopted any one of us. I remember that I was coloring in one of my books that life altering night, I loved coloring books when I was little…staying in the lines was so important to me. (That's probably how my OCD started!) I hated when my pain in the ass little brother scribbled on one of my pages. I don't recall where my brother and sister were that night. All I remember that it was just me and my daddy and

CUPCAKE

I was happy coloring away in my book. I remember I was working on a unicorn's head. It was some kind of princess book and I loved horses and of course unicorns, I was six! I was sitting on the floor on a big brown braided rug, at an old coffee table, meticulously working on my unicorn masterpiece. Then all of the sudden my daddy comes from behind me and yanks the book out from under my hands and my crayons fell on the floor! He startled me, but I didn't think I did anything wrong, so I wasn't thinking I was in any trouble and getting a spanking or anything. In a nice, calm, and strangely sweet voice he asked me if I'd like to play a game with him and if I did, and I did it good, I could have *chocolate cupcakes*! Now you have to understand that we were dirt freakin' poor and THAT was a treat that I hadn't had in a very long time! We couldn't afford real food...I practically turned into a can of spam for God's sake! So of course I eagerly said "Ok daddy!" He tossed my book on the couch, picked me up, and carried me upstairs to his and mommy's bedroom. I don't remember thinking anything was wrong or I was to be worried or scared at that point. They had the big bed. We children always had twin beds that were either up as bunk beds or both down on the floor which sucked because it took up far more space in the already cramped rooms. So he proceeds to put me down at the side of the bed and told me the first part of the game was I had to take off my clothes and crawl under the covers as fast as I could. I looked up at him, surprised I'm sure, and told him, "No, I don't want to." He said well if you don't, you won't get the cupcakes. I started to get a little upset and he knelt down in front of me and said, "Don't worry, it's ok! This is a fun game and you can have the cupcakes right after, I promise!" I was still upset but I REALLY wanted those cupcakes and it was even better when he reminded me that *I* was the only one getting the cupcakes because my brother and sister weren't there to play the game. So he said it one more time. "All you have to do is get undressed really fast and get under the covers before me and you win the game and you can have your cupcakes". I said "ok". I was six and just wanted those damn cupcakes. He said "ok, when I say go...do it as fast as you can!" He said it, I already didn't have shoes on...just socks...then I had brown corduroy pants with elastic at the top that my mom made...a turtleneck sweater with stripes...and my panties...they were pink and briefy things, nothing sexy...I was six! I went as fast as I could, stumbling around to try to become the first one done. He was on the other side of the bed and I thought I was winning! All my clothes were in a lump on the floor...my pink panties on the top of the pile and I jumped up on the bed and got under the covers as fast as I could! I won! I was the first one there! I yelled "I did it, I did it!" He then proceeded to slide into the bed never exposing himself from the waist down...the covers hid the lower part of his body. I sat up and said "Ok! I win...can I have my cupcakes now?" He quickly grabbed me by the waist and pulled me to the middle of the bed to him...and I could feel he didn't have any clothes on. I was cold...the bed was cold...and he was strong and had a hold on me...and I got scared as I felt his hairy skin touching mine. I started to cry and he said "The games not over yet...don't cry...it's ok! Some daddies and their little girls take baths together! The other part of this game is easier than that! We just need to roll around on top of each other for a minute and keep the covers on us, and then the game is over! Then you can get dressed and you can have your cupcakes!" I cried harder and said I didn't want to play anymore and he held me tight with my back to his front and rolled...more like rocked around the bed for a minute back and forth...side to side. I was crying and he kept reassuring me the game was almost over and I won and could have my cupcakes. I clenched my fists to my face real tight, as tight as I could and pulled my knees up to my chest as tight as I could. I didn't care about the stupid covers falling off. I wanted to fall off. He finally let me go. I darted out of the bed, fell on the floor and started to put back on my panties. I was crying. I knew my heart was racing and I was starting to calm down. I accidently put my panties on inside out wrong... (As I still do sometimes still these days)...and he tugged on the back of them and told me to "take them off again"...I started to cry again...and he said to "turn them right side out", they were on wrong. I thought I was going to have to play the game I didn't like again. I got dressed the right way as fast as I could and ran down the stairs and grabbed my book. My pretty unicorn page was ruined because he pulled it from me and the crayon went outside the lines. I started to cry again. He came downstairs a couple minutes later as I sat on the couch crying. He sat next to me, *made* me look at him and he said "I promised you your cupcakes, now I'm gonna go get them, you won fair and square but you *have* to promise me something, can you do that?" I said "What?" He told me "You can have your cupcakes but you *HAVE* to **promise me you won't tell mommy** about our special game." I sat still as could be for a minute and replied "ok, I promise." He took me into the kitchen; I hopped up on a ripped vinyl covered kitchen chair at the table and waited for my cupcakes. He reached way up high in a wooden slate blue painted cupboard and took down the box of cupcakes…the chocolate ones that had chocolate icing then that cool swirly design of white icing on top. I was soooo excited! Sad, I know…I was six! He knelt down, unwrapped the package of two held one out to me, looked me straight in the eyes, then grabbed my arm squeezing it tightly and said very firmly…"Remember…DON'T tell mommy, ok?" I said ok of course and grabbed the first one and shoved probably half in my mouth in one bite as if I had not had anything to eat in days. I wasn't quite finished with the second one and mommy came home from Bingo. She asked, "Why are you still up?! It's past your bedtime and why are you eating cupcakes this late at night?!" My dad said "She was a very good girl while you were at Bingo so I gave her a treat." I just looked up at my mom as she took off her jacket and shook my head up and down meaning yes, I was a good girl…I was still stuffing the cupcake in my face so I couldn't say a word if I wanted to. I don't even remember if I wanted to say something or not. I just wanted to eat my damn cupcakes.

By the way, I have nothing against the companies that make those cupcakes. I still see in almost every grocery store today…I just have never in 40 plus years have been able to have them again.

CHAPTER 3

The "Boogey Man" is Real

I CAN'T REMEMBER how much time had passed in between the first encounter in now becoming "a victim of sexual abuse", which was basically unheard of or at least NEVER talked about openly back in those days, and the second, and the third encounters. I do recall the second time being again where I was left alone in the house with him.

I remember I didn't realize I was alone and my mom was already gone. And I yet again, did not know where everyone else was. It was still day time though, and he came to me as I was upstairs playing with a doll in my room that I shared with my sister. He walked in and said "hey Katelyn, whatchu doin' up here all by yourself"? I just kept playing with my doll's hair and said "nothing". I thought I may have been in trouble for something? I didn't know yet that the house was empty besides him and me. He walked past me and pulled the curtains closed. They didn't block out the light from outside completely but it got dark enough that I looked up at him wondering why the heck did he just close the curtains??? I asked "where's mommy"? He said she went to the store. He didn't say what kind of store or how long she would be gone. He said it was time to play "our secret little game" again. I kept playing with my doll...now holding on to her harder than before and I knew my heart was pounding faster and it felt like it was going to pound out of my chest. I became really scared, really fast. I didn't want to look at him but I said "I don't want to" and I know he could hear the fear and hesitation in my voice. He went over and closed my door. He said it would be different this time and I'd really like it. He said I could have anything I wanted down in the pantry cabinets and he would get me a new "Barbie" doll if I'd say ok and play with him. I say "Barbie" in quotations because I didn't have the "real Barbie" dolls. Like I said, we were dirt flippin' poor and I had the knock off dolls or I got my sister's dolls when she didn't want them anymore. So now I was a becoming very upset but yet again, fell for the bribery tactics of the son of a bitch who manipulated me, a child that just turned six, into getting naked alone in my room this time, reluctantly, once again with him. I remember him lying on my bed which was a twin sized bed, properly aligned against the wall in front of the window. I also remember that he started to do some sort of bench presses with me, using my body like a weightlifter may use dumb bells or free weights. He was acting like he was Superman, and making me fly above him as he held me up above him. And this was the very first time I saw *it*...this big penis... (It seemed big to me because I was a small child)... and yes, unfortunately I was exposed to his hairy balls. I didn't know what exactly they were called at the time back then...I was six! All I knew was that my little brother had a little "wee-wee" or "pee-pee" and little "nuts" (because my mom said boys hurt there if you crack them in their "nuts") and I didn't have these things. I say big penis because I was six! Lots of things seem big when you're six. He was not a tall man; he was what was referred to back in the day as "husky" or "stocky" but I knew "it" scared me. It scared me unlike anything else I could imagine at that point. A six year old should be afraid of scary movies or spiders and bears. I should have been afraid to get a spanking for fighting with my sister or to get the belt for not cleaning up after supper. Anything, anything but some freakin' set of a grown man's genitals. I would have welcomed a few welts across my bony ass in place of his disgusting body touching mine. I remember feeling his abrasive yet hardened genitals against my butt cheeks during the last *game* we played and his pubic hair felt like "Brillo". I would help my mom with dishes so I knew what a Brillo pad felt like, it was not a pleasant sensation. I do not care for the texture of Brillo and that reference to his genitals is haunting. Needless to say I use nonstick pots and pans, I won that war. Wow! Such a triumph, right? Sickening how something so minor has to affect an innocent act like doing the damn dishes isn't it? Fuckin' asshole has to have a negative impact on so much in my life to this day.

So back to the nastiness of the genitals on the man who called himself my stepfather. I doubt any men shaved and groomed that entire area back in the 70s? Hell most of the women probably did not shave anywhere back then either! Anyway, I had a mixture of crying and giggling goin' on. I am an extremely ticklish person and he was "flying" me around kind of fast, and it would make me giggle, and at the same time I was crying because I was scared. It was now to the point of me crying and sort of squealing. I was yelling in this high pitched voice for him to "put me down! Put me down, I wanna get down"! He told me to stop acting like a baby and stop crying. He said "this ain't so bad is it"? I just wanted to be let down. He clearly was not happy with my reaction to his new *fun* game as his voice was changing. His voice and words were getting firmer and louder, telling me over and over that I was a big baby for crying over nothing. He was grunting and growling like a fuckin' disgusting animal as he continued to force me to play his game.

So, he went back to the bench pressing thing and please forgive me for being so graphic...I warned you, and it will get worse...but "flew me" up towards the top of his head and lowered me down slow as he stuck out his tongue and tried to get in between my legs! Who the fuck does this to a six year old little girl who looks NOTHING like a grown woman!?!? Maybe that's why I never really understood why grown women today shave or wax completely because #1 it's actually not healthy because the main purpose of hair is to trap bacteria and you need some down there to keep out bad bacteria from your coochie...even if it's a trimmed little landing strip...it still serves the health issue. Then #2…I would be weary if a grown man asked me to shave or wax completely…baby smooth because think about it, why would they want your coochie to LOOK like a freakin' child's coochie??? Hhhmmm…makes you wonder, doesn't it? I mean even teens have some pubic hair. It's part of distinguishing a child from an adult, is it not? So anyway, I was squirming around trying to wiggle myself out of his hands which were still holding me up some and I did not even care if I hurt myself and fell! He kept asking me, "doesn't that feel good, don't you like that!?" Like I was gonna scream YES with excitement or something??? WTF! I was kicking and shaking around yelling "NO! PUT ME DOWN!" over and over 'til he finally just kinda tossed me to the floor. I do not remember if I got hurt anywhere, but I was just soooo happy to be on the floor at that point I wouldn't have cared if I had broken a bone! I remember I ran across the hall into the bathroom and slammed the door. He kept asking if I was ok, I told him I had to pee. He just said "get dressed when you're done and come downstairs and remember, *don't tell mommy, you promised!*" I honestly don't remember what happened after that. You'll hear that often in my story because according to a therapist, I would remember certain things that just had such a strong impact on me as a child, so traumatic, it makes other details unmemorable by comparison. So there is A LOT that I will not be sharing with you all because *twelve years* and such frequency of the abuse would never completely be able to be documented. The thought of keeping a journal or a diary had never crossed my mind I guess because it started when I was so young and I didn't even know what a journal or diary was. And I just "blocked out" and suppressed a lot of incidences I am told, and probably for the best and for my own well being. Little bits and pieces surface in nightmares sometimes, but I am not sure if these acts or references of the sexual abuse actually happened or are just flat out nightmares occurring because I was sexually abused. So I only write about the things I know. If I second guess something, I will state just that.

CHAPTER **4**

Scared Shitless and Living a Freakin' Nightmare

I DON'T KNOW if I ever got my "Barbie" doll, but I know from that point on *I was scared*. Scared enough to start being paranoid about when and where every other member in my family was going to be and I knew I NEVER wanted to be left alone with "Daddy Dearest" again. I always cried and wasn't a little liar when I was younger... cause if I did lie, and got caught we would (us kids) get a backhand or the belt, or a paddle with holes drilled through it, depending on the severity of the lie. I was a bleeder too. It didn't take much for me to get a slap in the face and my nose to bleed like Niagara Falls. A therapist had mentioned that the bloody noses could have started so easily because of the constant anxiety and fear I was enduring year after year and experiencing worsening sexual abuse. I believe no one really knows such things for certain, but it sure as hell makes sense in my case. I can honestly say I lived in CONSTANT fear of my now real life Boogey Man because even when others were around, I was worrying about what would possibly happen IF they DID go somewhere and I was left alone with him I had to keep quiet because I was afraid he would beat me on top of it. I this present day, am still being treated for severe muscle tension and taking meds for an anxiety disorder diagnosed by professionals when I finally decided to seek help and talk to someone about my "problem". And I thought of it as that, a problem. There's something wrong with *me*. Sure as shit yeah! Sexually abused for twelve years out of 30 at that point...damn straight something's wrong! I was told that your body can become "used to" certain behaviors when repeated enough and become a habit of sorts. For me being consistently uptight, terrified, and scared shitless year after year after year...well my body just doesn't know how to relax on its own. Meditation, yoga, herbal supplements, I tried all things imaginable to help me sleep nights and just relax. I would find myself lying in bed, stiff as a freakin' board as an adult, basically all my life. I tried different methods to help myself but nothing worked, not even alcohol which became a bit of a problem at one point in my life. I felt hopeless and I will talk about my abuse of alcohol as an escape mechanism more later.

I lived in this creepy "haunted" looking house in the boonies in the Poconos down the narrow winding road from a little Lutheran church. This is the same church where my mother had married the demon who is now destroying my life before it barely even got started.

CHAPTER 5

Never Judge a Book by Its Cover

I DON'T KNOW how long it took before the violence in these sick encounters took place, I know they happened often, several times a week. Sometimes daily, sometimes more than once daily. I knew they worsened and became more severe, more damaging to me as a person as time went on. In the mind of someone who is a sick bastard I guess it depended on whenever the "mood" struck him and if the opportunity was there for the taking. But I do know that it wasn't long before the threats started coming. Threats and beatings against me, threats that if I EVER told my mother or ANYONE else, he would kill them all. My mother, my brothers and my sister. By 1972 my half brother "Jr." was born. A spawn of the devil himself in my eyes. It's not his fault but it's very difficult to not be reminded of my stepfather if I see him, which isn't often AT ALL...or the sound of his voice even freaks me out because he sounds like his father. My relationship today is fairly nonexistent partly because of such things. I know it's not fair to my half brother, but it is what it is.

My "daddy" also threatened to kill me more times than I could count. Trust me; there were times when I wished he actually did. You see, at a young age I fought back. I was not about to just let someone do something, anything, to me that didn't "feel" right. If I knew I didn't do anything wrong...then *why was **I** being punished*??? What the hell did *I* do to deserve this unthinkable shit?!

As I grew a little older, and as he was forcing himself on me time after time after time, I would ask him, crying, kicking and screaming, "Why are you doing this"?! He would usually take some minor incident for example, "You told your mother you cleaned your room." Even though I did, he would find the smallest flaw and use that as his excuse. I ALWAYS did what I was told and beyond, I was not a handful to my parents, never sassed back, always cleaned around the house or did chores outside to keep busy and tried to stay away from my so called "father". Now when both of our parents were gone the sibling hell raising would take over for sure. It was physical, loud as hell, and damaging to either our bodies or the house would suffer. That may have been the only "normal" activity we had. Scary, isn't it?

Other times when he was attacking me he would say it was "because I love you, and this is how I'm letting you know how much I love you." I have goose bumps writing this, and feel ill in my stomach, knowing the *demented* definition of "love" this asshole was convinced of? He truly felt it was justified and convinced himself his sick behavior was out of "love"? Was it all calculated to try to fool a young mind? Only he has the answer to that question. I'm disgusted recalling such things honestly, but it needs to come to light.

So, yes. This skinny, scrappy looking little girl ALWAYS put up a fight. I knew I probably wouldn't break free from this animal, but I sure as hell kept trying. When I talk to certain people I feel close enough to open up to about this with finally now in my adult life, I tell them that if anyone wants to mess with me for whatever reason…fuckin' bring it…I fought off a grown ass man for most of my life and I may get my ass kicked, but I'll sure as hell fuck you up trying. Am I a psycho, no. Can I freak the hell out and go into a "psycho" mode? You better believe it. It happens naturally. I'll share some sad examples later with y'all when I discuss my husband with you. Oh the challenges abuse has brought me.

CHAPTER **6**

Dear Lord, Where are you?

I KNOW I wasn't baptized until I was 7 years old. If I remember correctly my brothers and sister were "blessed" all at the same time. My half brother was fairly newly born so I'm guessing my mom decided to include the rest of us to have this done because of him. I do remember always going to church when I was young. How young? I couldn't say. I would either go with my step-grandma who lived on the property in the bungalow behind the house, or I would walk by myself if necessary when I was "old enough", which I don't remember an exact age. Back then, we were allowed to roam around outside without parents worrying so much about being abducted by a stranger. Sad but ironically enough that may have been a blessing right there for me. Fuck, what a horrible realization to have about yourself.

I went to Sunday school. I went to the adult services as well, whatever I was allowed to do, and I did it. I joined the children's choir and also became an acolyte for the church. I guess I thought lighting the altar candles and every other activity and having to spend more time up the hill at the church would bring me closer to God and he would answer my prayers, my questions, and save me. I threw myself to the mercy of the Lord to try to understand why these evil things were happening to me. I didn't understand what I possibly could have done to deserve what was happening to me. And I thought it was happening

ONLY to me. I prayed for so many crazy, bad things. I guess that alone was actually sinning. I prayed for him to die. To die in soooo many horribly painful ways I should be ashamed for, but I am not. I prayed for the Lord to make him leave my mom even though I figured she would be sad. I prayed for him to be struck by lightning. I prayed a big black bear would tear him up when he was hunting. I prayed and prayed and prayed. Later I'll tell you of my wondrous dreams of all the different yet delightful ways I would want to kill him myself if I had been given the chance, the chance to get away with it, that is. I even prayed for God to take me. I definitely wanted to die at times. I have no clue what kept me going when I was younger. I think at this point I was probably about 8 years old. I'd like to say it was my faith in God that kept me "quiet" and kept me living and still enduring the awful torture put upon me, but I can't. I knew God wasn't answering anything. Was he listening? Did he not care? Was he too busy with sick people? Did he even really exist? What "God" would let this happen to a child??? I was losing hope. I was losing faith.

I guess I was about 11 years old when I found a "friend" or two through the church. I at this point was NOT the outgoing type. NOT what you would call a fun loving, happy and "normal" kid. I was quiet, reserved, and mysterious to others I'm guessing because I never had too much to say unless called upon. I was NOT a social butterfly. I WAS a true introvert. I remember I grew my hair and insisted to not have bangs. My mom would always try to force barrettes and bobby pins on me to keep my side parted hair from covering my face. She'd yank at it and say, "Get that damn hair out of your eyes and off your face, you look like fuckin' Veronica Lake". I didn't know who the hell that was, but I knew it wasn't meant as a compliment for sure because she was always pissed when she would call me that. I just wanted to be invisible. She eventually cut my hair and gave me bangs, ugh, what a disaster with the home haircuts and hairstyles! It was obvious I was from a "poor" family. I wanted no one to see what I was feeling, not like anyone was guessing. I was ashamed of my house, our cars, my clothes, my family and myself. I never thought or felt pretty, despite what my stepfather would say. His so called opinion didn't mean jack shit to me. He said anything and everything to manipulate me to do what he wanted. I was never willing to do any of his nasty deeds, I had no other options, and my life was shit.

We'll call one of the girls I became friends with Winnie. She lived in a very nice brick one story house half way around the block. It was a big house with a really nice yard all around it. A place I could only dream of having one even close to hers someday. A "block" in the Poconos where I lived was about 4-5 miles around. Everybody had property and no one was there in plain view through your windows, not in our neck of the woods. So "Winnie" and I hung out at her house every now and again, studied some together and went to the same church. I think her mom was a seamstress and her dad did some form of sanitation with pumping sewers. Cleaning out other people's shit was profitable and a good living back then, probably still is. There should be no shame in that. Someone has to do it, right? So I hope those that do, get paid very well. ☺

All I know is she had a beautiful house in which I was allowed to visit, but she was never allowed over my house. Was it because of how it looked, so creepy, maybe her mom felt it was unsafe structurally, or filthy dirty inside? I don't know. (It *was* always clean by the way because of me, I'll tell you that!) Well, there came a time when a handful of us from the neighborhood block and surrounding area, had religion classes. They were required in order to be "confirmed" and become a member of the congregation. I think that's how it went. So anyway we had a religious "retreat" with the Pastor of the church and my class one weekend. I don't recall where we went, what it was called but it was on a big lake. There was a cabin, we had sleeping bags, and we grilled hot dogs and hamburgers…like camping. There was a dock and a little boat with oars. I wasn't the best swimmer, never was and I'm still not. I was always hesitant to get into the water. I was too old for a floaty donut, so I would just kind of hang in the water up to my chest clinging on the ladder attached to the dock. The other kids knew I was afraid of the water and respected that and never poked fun at me for it. I was thankful for that because at that age it was embarrassing. I remember having worn a two piece bathing suit. I had a stick as far as any body shape or having any curves, no boobs yet. Winnie on the other hand was a little heavier than me and had already started to grow her breasts. She was allowed to wear a "training bra". I always thought, train for what??? I grew to realize their purpose was to get a developing young girl used to wearing an added piece of clothing, never sure about that but I knew I couldn't wait to have one. (Now I can't wait to take the damn thing off!)

So anyway, most of the time our Pastor would just kind of linger around, monitor us but not suffocate us, give us a little space. He was pretty much letting us have our fun as kids on a retreat, as he should. We all got in our bathing suits and went for a swim (this is the second day), later in the morning after a breakfast of Lucky Charms. (Well I went for a "hang", while the rest swam). Winnie swam back to the dock and was holding on to it gently next to me. We were both in our two piece suits and Pastor Ray came walking out with his coffee mug and squatted down to chat with us. I cannot for the life of me remember what he was saying because I was so focused on how *his* eyes became focused on Winnie's breasts and how her topped became a little loose up top, it kind of bagged out a bit. I couldn't believe it! Our "Man of God", a freakin' peeping pervert himself! If he had gotten any closer and looked down her top any harder, his holy ass would have been in the lake head first right on top of her! I bet he would have loved that! I couldn't watch the piggish Pastor any longer and said "Winnie! Let's go for a walk, I'm starting to feel like a prune" as I held out my wrinkled soggy fingers. I rudely interrupted "Pastor Ray" in whatever the hell he was babbling/preaching about. I'm sure as shit it wasn't any of the commandments, and I didn't care that my actions could have been interpreted as disrespectful either. I was pissed. Winnie looked at me like…what the hell is your problem

"DON'T TELL MOMMY"

as she said if I really wanted to get out and go for a walk she would go with me. I got out and grabbed my towel as well as hers and gave it to her with a sense of urgency. She asked if I was ok. I just told her I had to pee and told her I couldn't do it in the lake like everyone else. Pastor Ray just got up and sat at a picnic table near the dock. He watched us dry off the whole time and as we walked to the cabin to change. I was so relieved he didn't follow us back! When we were inside in our room I told Winnie what I saw. She didn't believe me at first, trusting that he would never do something like that, and was like "EEWWWW"! I told her to just stay aware of what he does and watch who he pays more attention to and he will prove to be a perv to her all on his own. Sure enough, we both started observing how he never really paid much attention to the boys at all. He sure made the time to sneak around and chat with the girls though! We couldn't stop talking about it and we warned the only other girl with us, "Lauren", of what we thought we had discovered. We were all creeped out and stuck close to each other and stayed out of arms reach of the Pastor the rest of the retreat. He had asked us why we were so quiet. We just said we were tired from all the stuff we had been doing. We were definitely ready to go home. For me, I wasn't sure what was worse. I never wanted to be home but now there's another man I couldn't trust and HAD to be around, at least until my religious education had been completed. Sad thing is he was married and had a son. I left the church and Winnie told her Mom and she left after our confirmation too. We saw each other in school but never hung out much after that. Winnie's mom must have reported Pastor Ray to the church because my step grandmother told me he had left the church and moved out of the county not long after my confirmation. Winnie and I never discussed it, as things of that nature back then just *didn't* get discussed.

So now what do I do? I had thrown myself into the church and kept praying all kinds of crazy things to God and now my faith in him had dropped like a hot potato. I felt my prayers weren't being answered. He wasn't listening to me. I wanted to know *what the fuck I did to deserve all this ugliness in my life and why the hell I have no one to turn to now!* I felt so lost and alone. All I had learned to this point about this *God*...this "great spiritual being" who was supposed to watch over children, and where was he when I, a child needed him to save me? I was now starting to fall apart. I had lost faith and became more scared and tortured as each day went by.

CHAPTER **7**

School Became My New Savior

BY MIDDLE SCHOOL which was about age ten for me, I had been doing very well in school academically. I did so well and was actually bored with the work given to me that I was tested for the "gifted" program. The gifted program is what they call "AP", college prep, advanced classes these days as you are labeled by how high your IQ is when submitted an IQ test. I was so happy to qualify with ease and I was placed in these advanced classes which was at least something, the only thing at that point, sadly, the only thing positive in my life. I didn't have to study for tests but I was always asking for extra credit work or even more challenging materials just to keep myself busy at the house. I figured it would be a good excuse in my begging and pleading for him to leave me alone and not touch me. I would lie to him and say I had sooooo much homework to do, and if I didn't get it done I would get bad grades and mom would start asking questions. I knew he didn't want my mother to ask questions. But I really didn't and it didn't stop him, ever. Despite his constant drive to force me to do whatever sick act he had planned for me, I was thankful just knowing I had brains. I was a smart girl and I held on to that for dear life. I didn't think of myself as some dumb blonde that wasn't smart enough to stop the dumb ass, fuckin' probably inbred, redneck, that lived in the same freakin' house. I'm sure I thrived in my school work to escape the dreadful drama of my so called home life. I do try to find *anything* positive, still today as a grown woman that came out or will eventually will come out of all the inexcusable, horrific abuse I survived after twelve long years. Will I ever understand? No. There will always be too many unanswered questions…and you're about to find out why. And still no one knew, *or did they?*

CHAPTER 8

Silence Isn't Always Golden

FOR ROUGHLY FOUR years now I was a sexual play thing, a punching bag, a puppet, a humiliated being forced into submissions to my stepfather, and still, I was above all else, a child. I had never felt so alone. I never confided in ANYONE my *dirty little secret* that plagued my soul. The beast within the home on Millhouse Drive was becoming more vicious and forceful than ever. He made me believe that without a doubt, that he would kill my entire family if I breathed one word of what unthinkable sins he was bestowing upon me. There were too many times to count when I said I wished I were dead, or I wanted to die. I thought maybe God would take care of that in a kinder way back then. I thought God would set me free from all the pain and fear this *so called man* burdened me with. A man does not do such things to a child, only a demon would even engage in the slightest thoughts. Yet, I still could only scream the truth on the inside. I kept silent. Who would believe such things anyway? My mother... who married this *wonderful young man* who was willing to take her hand, raise and support her and her three children? My mother who was not able to be around as much as she had liked because she had to work two jobs to help make ends meet. My mother, who would have been heartbroken, mortified and at the very least enraged to find out that the man she married not only was taking her hand in marriage, but was taking the innocence of her children as well. If he didn't kill her, knowing that then would have.

How about someone at school? Could I confide in anyone there, and tell them that my own so-called "dad" was touching me in ways that I knew were wrong and disgusting? Hell no. No one talked about this sick shit back then! And I was young, blonde, yet far from dumb remember, and I knew better than that! I truly believed he would follow through on his threats and kill everyone.

Any friends? How about a close friend? I didn't have too many *close* friends at that age. I suppose it was due to the lying and lack of appropriate social skills it would take to acquire such relationships. I lied about lots of things at this stage in my adolescent life because I was embarrassed by my house and I was just afraid to have anyone close in fear of them finding out that dirty little secret. I didn't dare.

What about an aunt or uncle? The only "family" around was that of the same spawn in which he came from. I couldn't even think of telling on him to his own family. I felt that they would never have believed me, I'll never know for sure. It wasn't an option. I couldn't risk being responsible for the possible spilling of my own family's blood.

What about my older sister, Maureen? She was close to my age. We fought like siblings did when they were young. We would often beat the crap out of each other, pulled hair out, threw stuff at each other, and stole each other's clothes and shoes if they fit. We had our little rivalries, but it didn't seem to be anything monumental and wasn't a big deal to me. The seemingly usual relationship as other sisters would have. She was always sort of jealous of me and I'm not sure why to this day. My mother seems to think Maureen thought my parents *favored* me over her, maybe because I was younger? So what about Maureen? I'm asking you as the reader this…up 'til this point…had you asked yourself the

◄ **"DON'T TELL MOMMY"**

same question???

What you're about to read is probably one of the hardest parts of this book for me to write. But unfortunately it is necessary, because it happened and it is pure truth.

CHAPTER 9

Honor Thy Sister?

I HAD OFTEN asked myself the why me? Why me? Well my first recollection of my suspicions of my stepfather molesting my sister at all started growing stronger as I grew older. Then the unthinkable, the unforgivable happened. I was still ten; maybe eleven by this time and a highly disturbing, SHOCKING, awakening, a rough awakening had fallen upon me.

I was in my room and the door flew open and there he was...my worst nightmare once again. He dragged me into his room by my one arm as I was kicking, slapping, screaming, and crying. I don't know where everyone else was at that time. I know my mom was working, and I thought my sister was home and my brothers were out up on the property at my step grandparents' bungalow. My stepfather had stripped me down after throwing me down on the bed, as he's done several times before. He then took off his clothes and kept telling me that I needed to shut up because it didn't matter that I was loud, he didn't want to hear me being a big baby. I couldn't help myself as usual, crying uncontrollably and I would cover my eyes so I didn't see his nasty, naked body. I started kicking at him as he came within my reach. I slapped, punched, squealed with extreme distress and panic. I also begged, pleaded, and tried to reason with him to let me go. It wasn't an option. He was determined, as always, to put me through yet another night of pure hell. He slapped me at my hands which were still covering my face. I had my legs crossed not once but twice wrapped so tight that they were like a twisted pretzel stick. He yelled at me to "roll over, roll over, damn it!" And I just kept crying and yelling "No! Please stop, let me go!" It took a few times before he could get me over on my stomach on the bed as I started kicking again. (I was *always* putting up a frantic fight to keep him off me.) I fuckin' freaked each and every time! (My skin crawls and I am sickened just thinking back, seeing it in words on my laptop, of that disgusting sick bastard and *all* the gross shit he did to me.) So now he has me on my stomach and he is prying my legs apart. He is on his knees wedging himself to keep them apart. He said "Fuck!" as he leaned over the side of the bed and pulled out his GIANT jar of Vaseline from under the bed. (He always had that within reach in his bedroom, depending on what his plans were in how he was going to molest me I guess.) He pried my legs open again and I was still crying, lying on my stomach. He slapped my ass and told me to "Shut the fuck up already, it's not going to help!" I never stopped crying. I fuckin' hated him. He gooped his penis up with Vaseline and laid himself on top of me as I was face down. He began to rub his yucky dick at the top of my butt, rubbing it around the small of my back. I wasn't sure where this was going...literally! I do know I was scared out of my mind! I started to panic and flailed around like a fish out of water not realizing I could have made the situation go real bad by doing so, but thankfully "it" didn't go *there*. I guess he got frustrated enough with me because he backed off and got up. He slapped my backside once again and yelled at me again to shut up. "God damn, you're such a fuckin' cry baby!" He told me to move to the side of the bed and face him. He made me lay on my side. I was still crying and I did as he asked as I didn't want to be slapped anymore. When he would hit, he hit hard. It stung like hell. This was new. He had never asked me to lie on my side at the edge of the bed before. He stood near me and yelled..."Maureen, get the hell in here!" I thought I was hearing things! Maureen??? What? He's calling out to Maureen? What's going on?! I didn't say a word...I couldn't! I felt like it was hard to breathe as I was thinking what, how, why is he yelling for my sister?! I was whimpering like crazy. My crying had stopped in a state of bewilderness I suppose. I was so confused. And then I was shocked with an image that would never ever leave me. My sister appeared in the doorway. She didn't have any clothes on. Oh my gosh...she wasn't crying. I couldn't take my eyes off her. I didn't know what to think...about what was going on...about what was happening...about what was about to happen. She and the sick fuck in front of me exchanged words, but I'm not sure what was said. Even though they were right in front of me, their voices sounded like that of the teacher in the Charlie Brown cartoons..."wahnt, wahnt, wahnt" is the best I can describe it. It was blurred and I felt like I was in a REAL nightmare, was I imagining it all???

Unfortunately, I was not. It was as real as the anguish that still haunts me today. I'm guessing the words exchanged were my stepfather giving my sister some sort of instructions. I heard her voice as well but I don't know what she said, but she did what he asked and stayed near him, slightly behind him, off to his side. I was breathing heavy and my head was swirling. I felt whoosie, as if I were on a merry-go-round. My hands were in fists and tight to my chin as I still was trying to come out of my head spinning, regain some sort of focus and figure out just what the hell is going on. My dad... (Dad my ass), proceeded to focus on me as he demanded that I start to touch his *genitals*. I just looked at him, eyes full of tears and all was still blurry, and I just said, "Huh?" He yelled "You heard me!" I just looked at him. I was frozen. I couldn't move. I still felt like it was not real. I looked over at my sister with just a movement with my eyes only and *she just looked away from me*. I looked at Jared. He then proceeded to grab my left fist and pull my hand to his penis. He said, "Here, like this". I looked straight ahead at it. He had his one hand holding on to the base of his penis and held my clenched fist and started to move it back and forth in a stroking motion against the shaft. I felt the Vaseline on the tops of my fingers. Fuckin' gross! I wasn't about to open my hand. I was shaking, I still was in the shock of my sister being *right there*, in the same room, with him, with me, and naked! I muttered, "I don't want to do this" and he yelled "shut the fuck up you little bitch and open your hand!" He squeezed the hell out of my wrist until I opened my fingers. I kept my fingers limp and he really hurt my wrist. He stroked his penis with them again and continued to yell at me to "Grab it!" I started crying again and sort of forgot for a moment that my sister was there. I now had a task at hand…ugh…no pun intended, that was freaking me out even more, and I was not thinking about her. The more I resisted his commands, the more pissed off he was becoming. He swore at me more, and slapped me one more time. This time across my shoulder and I almost fell off the bed. I swore I heard my sister giggle. I was crying hard at this point and the yelling and swearing continued for a bit. He turned to my sister and said something to her and I heard her say "Ok". Jared then began stroking *it* himself and told me NOT to move. I put my hands back over my eyes, that wasn't something I wanted to watch. As he was *doing his thing*, I heard him start to make nauseating moans and groans. Oh my gosh, I surely wanted to vomit. It wasn't the first time he had made any disgusting noises, but it was the first time he was in front of me where I could see. It just made it sooo much worse in my mind. I opened my eyes, wiped my face and the clear drippy snot pouring out of my nose, which all saturated my skin with my hands real quick. As I had my hands away from my face for a moment I couldn't help but to see my sister's left hand fondling Jared's scrotum! The more she rubbed his ball sack, the more he moaned. Then he was putting his hands (swapping left and right with his penis) on her vagina and breasts, rubbing both clumsily, like if he didn't do it fast enough, they were going to runaway and disappear or something. I was really blown away by this image. Shocked, grossed out, dumbfounded, however you can describe the worst thing you can imagine seeing your sister do, or so I thought, that was it. (You'll find out what's worse later.) As you can tell it is forever scarred in my memory, as is all the harshest of acts which I have had to come to terms with. This was actually happening and I had no fuckin' control over it. I was helpless. What happens next is unforgivable. Not only did my sister NOT do anything to help protect her little sister from this animal, (that word is too kind for him), she was *assisting* him in the act…and she didn't seem to mind! …What the fuck!?!

I covered my eyes as fast as I could. Then that fast, Jared freed his right hand from his session of jerking himself off and smacked my hands away from my face and demanded I keep them down by my legs. I screamed as I was startled and closed my eyes as tight as I could. I wasn't sure what was going to happen next, and nothing could ever prepare me for what was coming soon. (Again, no pun intended. This is far from funny as you can see.) I heard the *icky* suction sound of him spanking his cock and his breathing became more frantic. I just kept my eyes shut, and a good thing I did. That fuckin' pig then climaxed and ejaculated on my face. Yes, I said on my face. Do you want to know the absolute worst part; it wasn't the act itself, but that my sister fuckin' laughed as he spewed his load all over my face. Yeah, she fuckin' laughed. Right there in front of me and all she said was "That was mean", as she laughed.

I immediately spit at them both as some of his smelly shit landed on my lips. I wanted to throw up and I was about to. It was hot and slimy and I will never forgive, never forget. It was rank in odor, now being so close that it was literally going up my nose. That's a stench you never forget. I started to cry but had to clench my lips so tight so his sperm wouldn't get in my mouth. Snot was shooting out my nose, I began to cough, choke, and wail with screams, as if someone had their hand over my mouth. (I wished it was just someone's hand.) That was by far, the most humiliating day in my life thus far. And to find out my sister was experiencing the same "abuse" as I was…but realizing she may have actually liked it…then managing to partake in the nastiest sexual act (I feel besides anal sex, that's just my opinion, to each their own.) nastiest that a man can do to someone…I seriously just wanted to die.

"DON'T TELL MOMMY"

Jared told Maureen to grab the towel (he had prepared prior), and she picked it up and gave it to him. He wiped his slimy dick off with it, then threw it *at* my face and yelled at me to clean it off. I was crying hysterically, gagging and choking, as I got up. I was bent over ready to puke on the big blue braided rug on the bedroom floor. The towel was wet and smelled like all his nastiness. It was difficult to find a clean, dry spot for me to wipe my face off. I used the corners and did the best I could. I took off running out the door, across and down the hall, then into the bathroom. I slammed the door, there wasn't a lock. I prayed no one would follow me into the bathroom. I looked in the crackled mirror over the vanity. I saw his sperm in my hair. I let out some hellish crying, it was uncontrollable. I immediately went to the bath tub, (we didn't have a shower, some fuckin' plumber, we didn't even have a shower in the freakin' house!), and I started to run the water. It was cold for a while but I got in anyway. I got in the tub even before I cleaned it, I never did that. There were now six of us sharing one tub, gross. I was quick to splash water in my face, hot or not and stick my head under the faucet to wet my hair. I loaded up the Prell shampoo my mom bought for us girls to use and started *scrubbing* like I had a pile of dirt from the garden in my hair. When I was all lathered up I grabbed the bar of Ivory soap, (I liked it because it floated in the bath water), and I lathered up my face not paying attention to the suds getting into my eyes. I was usually very careful not to get soap in my eyes or water in my ears. It drove me crazy if I did, I still hate it to this day. I didn't care that my eyes were burning as my hysteria continued. I felt so dirty. I felt dirty even after being in the tub for a long time. Definitely longer than usual anyway. I sat there until the water accidently drained on its own because I was so shaky when I started the water, I didn't plug the drain properly. I was used to hearing someone yell at me to get out of the bathroom because there were so many of us that needed to use it. They left me alone. I heard them moving around upstairs still. Then I heard them talk about getting ice cream out of the basement freezer as they went down the steep staircase to the first floor, then someone went down into our basement for what? Some cheap ass brand of *celebratory* fuckin' ice cream? Are you kidding me??? I was now going from hysteria to anger. I jumped at the opportunity to get out and get ready for bed and just sink literally, into my bed. I did so even with my hair wet. I never did that either. I wore footy pajamas; I wore them up into my teen years, for more than warmth. I felt a little more protected I guess, the less skin showing, the better. So I would wear them until they had worn so much they were ready to fall off! I was always cold anyway. I leaped into bed and pulled the covers over my head. I went into the fetal position, which was the only way I could usually fall asleep. I listened for my mother to come home from work. It felt like it was late. I wasn't sure what time it was, we didn't have the luxury of an alarm clock in our room. The last thing I heard that frightful night was my now known, betraying sister. She opened our bedroom door and yelled at me, "You didn't clean the tub!" Really? That's fuckin' all you have to say to me? We haven't *been right* in our relationship as sisters since. I was crushed and I was angry, words can't describe how hurt I am and the pain I feel. Any trust in her was now gone, with anything, with everything. After that she acted as if nothing ever happened. We became strangers and enemies. I felt hatred for her every time I had to look at her. I can't be around her even today as a grown woman. Like I said, can't forgive, at least not at this day in my life, and I sure as hell can never forget. I make excuses for her in my own mind and blame it on Jared, but she never came to terms with the abuse or deviant acts she participated in.

You will learn there are many theories, but never any answers as she refused all her life to talk about it…to anyone. She lost her baby sister at the door and doesn't realize it, or just doesn't give a fuck.

CHAPTER **10**

Dirty Deeds

I HAVE BEEN contemplating in which direction I should take you, the reader, next. Do I focus on the positivity, although so limited in my life at a young age, or continue with the somewhat shocking and grotesque acts in which I endured. Having already disclosed one of the most difficult disgusting facts about my sibling, to whom I never would have expected to become the obviously highly influenced, evil tempered creature she demonstrated, I decided to continue the shock factor flow of some of the *dirty deeds* that were forced upon me. I guess to kind of get the bulk of this awful information out of the way and allow you to realize there are *some*, not many, but some nice recollections and people who helped save me from myself back in the day.

I guess some of my earliest memories of how Jared attempted to groom me into his cute (or maybe even sexy in his eyes, ugh...yuck!) young puppet, sex kitten, whatever you would call a child who was being looked at and treated sexually as a woman. I call it freakin' crazy for one. Sick as hell barely begins to describe the churning ill feeling in my stomach as I write this. He would demonstrate and dictate to me *how* he wanted me to touch him. How I should be holding my hands. How I should lay on a bed or on the floor. How *I* should be gentle in my touch on his body or at times how I was to be rougher in certain acts, such as squeezing my hand harder on his genitals, you get the picture I'm sure. He was very specific and through all my kicking, screaming, and crying would never take NO for an answer. It meant punishment on me in different ways if I defied him, in which I always did. I never made it "easy" for him to put his hands or any other part of him, on me. I hated his very existence. I also knew I was stuck and at his mercy thinking and knowing him, to me, was very capable of killing all those in my family. I believed him. Then to top the nightmare off knowing my sister was basically on his side was devastating to me. I felt life was hopeless.

Jared would demand and instruct me even on the process of taking off my clothes. I, being reluctant and being a child, did not exactly have the smooth, seductive, sensuality of that maybe of some stripper. I guess that's possibly what he wanted? I can honestly say he never got that from me. To this day I have issues dealing with something as simple to most with the task, act, whatever you want to call it…of taking off my clothes in front of someone. It's very awkward for me, to have someone watch me disrobe…even at the age of forty seven. I want to be a "sex kitten" in that manner for my husband now but battle with the relationship to my past with having been commanded or else beaten, and have my clothes yanked off me by that asshole. He has ruined me and has made me afraid to be possibly the *free spirited* woman I yearn to be sexually with my husband. I am hoping that upon completion of this book and getting my story out there will unleash some inhibitions that have been held deep inside me for so long. I personally feel I am conservative sexually and I am very thankful my husband has the patience and determination to never give up on me and can romance me which allows me to feel at best decent about how I satisfy him sexually…he claims to have no complaints…I think he is just being kind, bless his soul!

I remember my stepfather using massage of sorts as an introduction to fondling and touching in an inappropriate manner. I learned at an early age that even a certain tone of his voice…I knew what was to follow. I found in relationships with guys at a later age...post high school...that massage was a "tactic" they too would use to relax me and it allowed them to put their hands on me and possibly have the massage go to a different level of physical activity. It took a long time for me to trust a male to even put their hands on me. (That is a whole other story to come later in the book.) Jared also would control any and all positions he wanted me to place my body into. These positions ranged from something seemingly simple as" just standing there", but in the nude...to a position more demeaning like getting on all fours like a common dog, and of course...naked. He would be what I claim is every man's characteristic of being visual in a sexual manner. I have come to know through my own experiences or I have been told by other women that men are visual creatures when it comes to sex. Hell even before they meet someone they have already envisioned themselves having sex with that person within the first five seconds! I heard that on TV! So as an adult I understand that aspect, just not that of a grown ass man wanting to view a child in that manner. Fuckin' PIGISH! I guess that's why more men are into pornography, or at least I hear of it being more common for men to view it than women, because they are genetically more visual sexually than women??? Whatever...but when it comes to visualizing kids in any sexual manner...it's <u>never</u> *natural or normal!*

There are some other associations or *triggers* that frustrate me as a grown woman because of what I was exposed to by this maniac as a child. It may sound silly but I would never buy or use Irish Spring bar soap or Ivory bar soap to present day. They are both fine products but because they remind me of my horrible childhood and how my stepfather would smell or taste when he forced me to give him oral sex, I can honestly say I would be physically ill if I were to come in contact with those soaps ever again. Then there is good ole Vaseline. The Vaseline in the giant tub with the blue lid. I am sooooo grossed out even seeing it on a store shelf. This was something my stepfather *always* kept under his bed and used to lube up his penis or parts of my genitals to molest me. Just the thought of the sloppy, gross, goopiness and texture of the shit. The sound it made while he had me jerk him off or while he did it to himself while he stared at me in a certain sexual position makes me want to vomit! One of the acts he forced on me was for me to get naked with him and he would position himself behind me on the bed. I was VERY young and he would take a gob of Vaseline and slap it between my legs and use it to lube up his penis and he would instruct me to squeeze my legs as close together as I could while he gyrated his filthy dick back and forth between my legs...touching my vagina, (which I didn't even know WAS my vagina because I was so young,) but not really penetrating my vagina. So he was just whacking off with us lying on our sides, or sometimes he would have me lay face down on the bed while he did the same thing. I now know that him doing that from behind in the manner and hostility in which he did perform that act sometimes could have gone really bad for my backside! If that did happen to me, anal penetration, I am guessing I would remember it because it would have been sooooo painful, especially at a young age but I can honestly say that I do not recall that happening. A therapist said such acts have a high level of severity that it is possible that some horrific things may have happened but I have blocked them out in order to save myself from having to deal with the reality of it actually have taken place. If that's the case, I am thankful for suppressing certain things and hope they never surface. How much could a child endure??? It's bad enough I remember all that I do. What doesn't kill you makes you stronger... ugh. It's true but I despise the source of what could have killed me.

If I wasn't performing as good as Jared would have liked me to, he would demonstrate on himself just how he wanted me to do it to him. For example, he would have me touching his nasty hairy ball sac while he masturbated, and of course we were naked. He would have to physically pry my arms and hands away from my body to get me to touch him. And then I would keep clenched fists. He wouldn't hesitate to slap the shit out of me in places that would be covered by my clothes so no one would see the welts, or yank me by my hair so hard my head would throb for a very long time. He did anything and everything, anything to get me to do what HE wanted. I was basically his sex slave??? I really thought I was the only one and I often wonder when he had started sexually abusing my sister. I may never know as she refuses to talk about it and admit that such horrible things even took place…things that she at one point willingly took part in. Things that she knew he was doing to me and didn't do a fuckin' thing to stop him and as a big sister…protect me. Do I want to know at this point? I don't think I can honestly answer that question even to myself. It's been soooo many years of bad blood…bad memories…I feel it, (my relationship with my sister) is well beyond repair. She's too fucked up and never came to terms with all this. It's pitiful and enraging at the same time. The only thing she has ever been driven to do is take advantage of people or situations in any way she could. Lies. She lies about anything and everything. I can understand as a child doing so, especially in our situation. I know I was embarrassed of a lot of things and lied to people while growing up. I hated my life and how I was. Being honest to others didn't seem to hold a top priority spot on my list back then. I am soooo opposite now. If you were to ask my own kids the question; what's the worst thing you could do to your mother? They would respond that the worst thing they could do to me would be to lie to me. I do believe I despise those who lie today because I lived a life of nothing but lies for so freakin' long that it was exhausting, stressful, and NOT the kind of person I wanted to be. I look down at those who lie and see no need for it. I have taught my children to be honest with me at any cost and I promised not to judge them and I honor that promise. I practice what I preach and I am damn proud of it. I take responsibility for my actions as a grown woman and look down on those who hide behind deceit and false securities just to make themselves and their lives look good…my ex husband can verify that one. (That whole heap of shit may be in my next book ☺.)

So anyway, what other twisted shit do I need to mention for those who think being "molested" isn't such a big deal because it's so commonly known these days? I shouldn't be sarcastic because I am so glad people actually started speaking out and standing up for themselves…and shame on you to those who make it up just for attention. There's that karma again. Oh trust me; it will get you every time. Amen to that. (I told you I had to have faith in something.)

Gestures. Let us talk a moment about gestures. Those of which some men think are sexy but in fact actually repulsing to a lot of women. Gestures like the motioning of their hand…extended flat and moving it up and down in a motion to mimic that of a scenario such as…"hey bitch…why don't you come over here and suck my dick!" Oh my fucking gosh! I can never forget how my stepfather would literally have to take his hands and wrap them around my head and force the motion of my head after he forced his cock in my little mouth to get a blow job from me as a child. Sick, I know. I hope all you men who read this realize how revolting that lovely gesture is next time before you try to *wow* your woman with your swag. It doesn't take a rape victim or a product of incest to be disrespected with shit like that. It is just not sexy and unless you are a pig and possibly a whore I would hope women find it a turn off when a guy goes all Andrew Dice Clay on them. (Sorry Mr. Clay, but I remember your work from back in the day to be disrespectful to women and the references insulting, that's just my opinion.) So forgive me if I want to cut off your balls and stuff them in your mouth if I were to see someone giving such a gesture. Trigger! I want to please my man. The last thing I want to do is be commanded to do it, considering my upbringing and all. I have to remind my husband of that from time to time. He forgets and I end up feeling bad. Bad because it should be completely normal and ok for my husband, being a man, to do stupid guy things like make a sexual gesture…to his wife…and his wife not get freaked out about it. But he can't, because I can't. And it's supposed to be all in fun but it gets turned into horrible flashbacks and throws me into what I call my *shutdown mode*. This is where all fun and giggles and shit get tossed out the fuckin' window because my fun loving husband innocently does something that my stepfather forced me to do as a kid and has basically tainted in my brain and psyche forever. Yes, rot in hell Jared, you son of a bitch.

Singing out loud is supposed to be fun and a great way to express joy, is it not? I grew up back in the days of eight track tapes and then later as I graduated high school in 1984 we had cassette tapes. There were still of course the vinyl albums and 45s that people would put on record players, or now referred to as turn tables. Well my family of course had the bottom of the barrel line of entertainment systems. The eight track tape player. There weren't any Elmo tapes or Barney or anything geared for kids…I don't remember having anything cheerful that made me happy, at least not in my family's shit hole of a house. Jared had his eight track player in his old black Ford truck. I remember some specific tapes he would play repeatedly. One was Johnny Cash and the other was Conway Twitty and Loretta Lynn. I also remember some Dolly Pardon and The Guess Who and of course Elvis. I guess that's all he could afford? I was pretty smart and listened to this stuff over and over and I memorized a lot of the lyrics. I remember hearing Jared sing to these tapes and artists, and he thought he had some voice I suppose. But it was like nails on a blackboard to me. I would cover my ears so I wouldn't have to hear him sing. The truck had a full bench seat in it so I had to sit on the passenger's side *without* a seat belt and be subject to a backhand when I did this every now and again. I sat as close to the door and window as physics would allow me to. I believe I just despised him so much that I felt he was ruining this nice music that was playing and I felt it wasn't something I wanted to listen to. Hearing him think he was a good singer. He would also tap, bang, slap, thump with his hands and fingers, whatever you would call it…the fake drummer wanna be shit that a lot of guys do…and off beat of course. THAT drove me insane! It still does! (My ex was the worse! Can't carry a tune or a rhythm in a paper bag!)

I had HATED country music growing up after all that. It wasn't until I met an old boyfriend as an adult and was introduced to Big and Rich that I gave it a second chance. I fell for their country rock sound and I believe that allowed me to ease into the world of country music as it is today. There will always be some triggers of the old school stuff, but that's not often and I have the freedom to at least turn it off now.

I know people should be able to express themselves through music and all, but Jared totally ruined the way I viewed people who do it without care…as it should be. I was critical and irritated and let him know he sucked at singing with my gesture of covering my ears. He would slap at me while he was driving and yell at me. He would say things like, "So you think you can sing better?!" "Okay Miss Fancy Pants…you sing then!" I would say I didn't want to and put my hands down from my ears but he would always get really pissed at me for making fun of him basically and it grew into me not really giving a shit because I was not about to say, "Oh daddy, you're the best singer ever!" Fuck that! He did slap me on a number of occasions when I would get cocky and not care and cover my ears. He would slap at me and threaten to pull over and pull down my pants and spank me if I didn't sing. Lord knows I didn't want him to pull over anywhere and I sure as hell didn't want him anywhere near my pants! I sang…sort of. It was more like muttering and slurring the words. At least I knew them…fuckin' dumb ass. (Man, I was little and I remember that… the first time that happened, like it was yesterday! And now I can't remember something I did 5 minutes ago sometimes!) So Jared would join in and sing and then say crap like "We sound pretty good together, don't we?" Hah! Together nothing! Ugh…I hated having to go anywhere with him. He has probably made me critical of myself and others in singing out loud with another person around. Yes, I blame him. Even though I joined chorus in elementary and middle school and I was in the church choir as well for some time, as I grew I became more reserved around others and didn't want to make a fool of myself singing like he did. I joined anything I could that didn't require money and it allowed me to be away from that house as much as possible. The whole singing thing may sound silly, but that's part of an inhibition I wished I had. I sooo feel like busting out into a song when it's a favorite but still at the age of 47 I find myself shying away and I kind of feel it goes back to that. My insecurities seem endless unfortunately. But I have faith that I will overcome. That is why you are reading this. You are helping me overcome by listening, and possibly sharing. More importantly I hope you are learning. And I honestly feel everyone should bust out in a song and dance and not give two shits about who hears or sees…let it go! Have at it! Express yourself…in tune or out! I think it's great if someone is out of tune and they don't care…karaoke is a blast for me to watch. I could never actually get up and do that…still too insecure and can't let it fly like I may want to.

I hope I can make some people appreciate the little things more… they are the best in life when you can enjoy them…so definitely embrace them!

Oh, what else has Jared done and destroyed for me…so much to choose from. I guess I could talk about those rides with him. From an early age I can remember Jared making me go with him to the store, or he had to go to the volunteer fire house to do something supposedly and he would make me go along. The only problem is that I remember that probably nine ride alongs out of ten, Jared would NOT go straight to our said destination or would NOT take the normal path to travel back. There were a few destinations off the beaten path off the winding mountain roads that he made his little *hideaway* spots for performing his sadistic acts on me or made me do to him. It was usually after dark, and I remember two spots in particular that I would start to panic if he started driving in those directions. Now remember this was in the 70s and there were tons of remote places a vehicle could be hidden from sight in the dark hours of night and no one would ever know someone was there. One was on the way to my cousins' house back Fountain Drive. He would take a side dirt road off of that Fountain Road and drive into the woods where no one would hear my cries for help. No one would ever know of what the sexual predator I knew as my stepfather was forcing me, a child, to do incredibly disgusting things to him. If anything they may have seen a vehicle using a spotlight looking for deer. He would keep a spotlight in the truck and we would go deer spotting from time to time with my siblings sometimes. The other that stands out in my mind was a dirt road off a road that went very steep up a hill to my Aunt Karen and Uncle Bernie's house. I remember it was like a roller coaster going straight up as you crossed over the intersection near where we lived. It was those rides that I was forced to go alone with Jared that I feared most. Even as I was in high school he would be waiting up at the bus stop where the after school activity bus would drop me, which was NOT far up the road from the house. I had no problem walking the short distance in the dark. To me it was better than being home alone or in a vehicle with Jared. I was thankful for being able to stay at school as long as I could. I knew when I saw him waiting there in the dark he was going to take me somewhere and force me to do things I didn't want to do. Things that I didn't know other people did. These nasty, dirty acts involving sexual behaviors that were meant for adults. I was in constant fear and anxiety always wondering if when I arrived at my bus stop or at my house…will that monster who tortured me be there waiting for me like some sick psychopath.

I know it took me a long time to trust a guy enough for me to let my guard down and admit and say" I love you" to them. My *stepdad* also forced me to say "I love you daddy" and give him a kiss at the end of his *sessions of filth* with me. I would be crying and shaking. It did not matter to him. I guess it made him think I was actually in agreement with the unjustifiable disgusting things he was doing to me??? There is no way in hell any sane person would believe a child who was hysterical and freaking out when they were near them alone would actually love them??? Fear doesn't begin to describe how I felt and he knew it. He used that fear against me yet needed to pretend it was ok for him to poke and violate me in ways I had never dreamed of…I was a child! I knew in my heart and my body that those encounters were not the way a father or a daddy was supposed to *love* their little girl. He was sick. A sick bastard and I fuckin' hated his very existence.

Sex is #1 *supposed* to be for the mature. Sex #2 is *supposed* to be something coveted and special. So special that you only share your body in the most intimate of ways that you *should* ONLY share it with someone you truly love, and are not fuckin' related to, by the way, just sayin'. I will always call it incest even if it's between step family members. Screw the definition. As far as I am concerned if I was to take on the role of becoming someone's stepmother, I would be taking ownership of sorts and treating, loving that child as if he or she WAS a blood relative. I feel some sick fucks use that as an excuse in their defense. That's bullshit and if you touch your stepchild inappropriately, you may as well be doing it to your biological child. That's my opinion.

So with this being said, Jared also stole my whole awareness of what real love and sexual behavior was. I was introduced to it and understood it as an act, not an emotion. An act of just going through motions to give men what THEY wanted. I had honestly not realized that fact until I met my current husband. I was with my first husband, the father of my children, for 16 years. We didn't get things right, on both ends.

I was in awe of him and he said "*I had potential.*" (Nice, I know… jack ass.) But the important thing is I did have two exceptional children and I learned a hell of a lot about relationships with men. It *doesn't have to be all about them!* Newsflash! What a liberating revelation! I sought therapy for my abusive childhood and I was able to come to terms with some things with that. But I feel it has been my life experiences and my knowledge I received from working with the general public that educated me most about how *REAL* love in life needed to be. I've met all kinds of people and I listened and learned. I found I was not alone. I was relieved and saddened at the same time. I no longer chose to *settle* for a man who had *settled* for me. I realized he was there because I was the mother of his children. Oh and let's not forget…"*I had potential".* Lucky girl, right? I was invested, the one, possibly the only one in love and was thankful he married me. No one should feel that way. No woman should feel so low about themselves that they choose false realities mistakenly for what they think love and sex should be about. I thought I was coming up in the world because I had married a guy who was a legend in his own mind and STILL lives in his "hey day" of high school. Who gives a shit? That was so freaking long ago and he should be embarrassed to cling to that to make himself feel superior. Care about the now! (Dumb ass.) That's how he lost me, not once, but twice. I tried to convince myself it was different the second time around. He was different from all the guys who basically took advantage of a young girl who thought sex was what she was supposed to just give a guy. It was expected. I thought it was how relationships worked. I'm not ripping on my ex husband. I am saying it took a long time but I did one day realize he was the right father for my kids, but not the right man for me. Egos run big in his family. There wasn't enough room for me, for him, and his enormous ego. I no longer agreed to pretend what we had was the real deal. I was doing once again what was expected of me, but I wanted more. I was ignored and felt used. I knew someday I would be writing this book. I am not invisible and I won't be that broken quiet child anymore.

I didn't know my first marriage would end and I would learn so much more about myself in my 30s. Jared will hopefully become just a part of my past, like those others I gave my body to not knowing it was truly wrong back then. It took a long time for me to take charge of my life and my body. I had to learn it was mine and I could have control even after all Jared had me programmed to think. There was hope. Hope I found when I found my current husband. Every woman should know their body is theirs and they should be the ones in control of it, not settle for a man just to say you have one, and give it away. Make the love and the sex count. Make it be special and have real meaning. That is one of the things I took from all the turmoil and torture and looking back I can't believe how far I've come. I am proud of myself.

I recall an incident when Jared had me cornered in my bedroom, one I ALWAYS had to share with my sister, and he pretty much ripped off my clothes and I was flipping out. It happened so fast I think it just took by breath away in panic and he wouldn't let me go. He was holding me by my hair with one hand and literally yanking at my clothes trying to rip them off without even trying to open a zipper on my jeans or undo any buttons on my shirt. I remember he let go of my hair…which was cut now at about my shoulders, and I liked to curl it like Farah Faucet back then, it was the 70s. So curling my hair and using some Aqua Net Hairspray made it puffier n thicker… easier for him to whip me around with. He let go of the grip he had on my hair and started working on the zipper as he realized finally that pants don't exactly come off without undoing them. What was he thinking and what the hell provoked him to come at me soooo freakin' hard and with such rage??? It was unprovoked on my part as far as I can remember and I recall yelling at him that "I didn't do anything and what's wrong with you, why are you doing this…I didn't do anything!" He grunted and was breathing heavily as if he had just ran an eight minute mile or something…he was pissed about something or at someone and was about to take his shit out on me! He was rough before. Some of his advances far more vicious than others. But I distinctly remember this time was off the chain as far as his temper went and I knew it was going to be real bad. As he finished yanking off my clothes, I was pulled down on the bedroom floor at this point, I broke free from him and ran out my door, down the hall, (we were in the far corner bedroom at this time…we would switch bedrooms around a lot, my mother still rearranges furniture weekly to this day, it's just something she has always done.) So I ran down the hall, whipped around the banister, which was getting pretty wobbly from all of us treating it poorly, and I flew into the bathroom and slammed the door shut. I pressed my naked body against it as hard as I could, like I could really stop him from busting through it. I weighed not even one hundred pounds at my age then, skinny as hell, and I heard silence. I was breathing hard, but I heard nothing. Did he come to his senses and decide to leave me alone for once? This had been going on for years at this point in time so it could happen, right? It surely was wishful thinking on my part. Fuckin' stupid on my part to even think he would even have a real heart let alone a change of heart. After about a quick minute he came slamming at the bathroom door that never had a lock on it, talking to me in an almost demonic voice saying "You fuckin' little bitch, you think you can get away from me? When will you learn you ain't never gonna get away from me? You just made this worse for yourself." It was a creepy calmer but deep tone in his voice and I remember I threw up some in my mouth and tried to swallow it back down but chocked on it instead. I knew I couldn't hold him out the door as he pushed the door open as if I was a suit jacket hanging on the other side…like nothing he burst in the bathroom pinning me behind the door and against the wall with the door. I'll never forget seeing his scruffy bearded little fuckin' troll like head peering through the gap between the door and the wall in which I was cowering behind in the small space. Straight out of a horror movie. A horror movie that I had never seen at that age but was living in my real life. Now the suspense movies with chases in them by psychos trying to kill women are the ones I have the hardest time watching, another trigger I suppose. I can watch the Saw series movies and be intrigued, but those where a woman or children are being "hunted" freak me the hell out!

So now at this point I'm trying NOT to look at him, and I knew whatever was about to happen to me was going to be unlike any other incident I had experienced in the past, I just knew it. I heard a "tap tap tap" on the door with something hard. I pulled my one fist away from one eye and saw his one eye glaring at me and then I also saw something dark in color he was wiggling and tapping on the door… it was a black revolver.

Holy crap is pretty much what went through my head! I'm pretty sure the moment I laid eyes on that pistol my heart stopped and I held my breath. No words can truly describe the first time someone pulls a gun on you, and I hope the majority of you reading this never have to experience anyone using ANY type of weapon and threaten your life for any reason. This is embarrassing but, I wet myself. Then I started crying and slowly sliding down in the corner still urinating and I pretty much was sitting in it in the tiny space behind the door against the wall. I couldn't think, I was frozen in fear and didn't know what to do. I don't think I did a thing. It was clearly his move. I knew nothing of self defense with weapons. I was still very young, in middle school, and I had gun safety training for hunting with a rifle, but not any training for what I needed at that moment. That moment now took this asshole's abuse to a whole new level. What was I to do? He called me out like that creepy child kidnapper in the classic movie Chitty Chitty Bang Bang…the weird candy man who had the black cape and top hat with the enormously hideous nose. I am still creeped out and haven't watched that movie since I was a kid. Another trigger? Probably so. Giving me goose bumps again! Ugh…horrible.

So Jared, daddy dearest, was saying creepy shit like "Come out come out little Miss Katelyn", in that voice, a perverted voice. "You know you can't hide from me. You are bringing this all on yourself so come on out now, ya' hear?" Ugh…was he high? I didn't know what that even meant back then…this is in retrospect…was he drunk? That wasn't unheard of. My mom says he never drank much, but when he did he got hammered! My mother referred to him as a lightweight when it came to drinking. I disagree with her there. I remember seeing him drink liquor or his homemade dandelion wine in a clear rocks glass. You would expect a Mason jar, and he probably had moonshine in our cellar too, I just didn't know what that stuff was.

So what the hell was his deal this time? I was soon to find out. He opened the gap in the door slowly and sure enough it was definitely a pistol in his hand that he was now handling very nonchallantly, like it seemed to be able to fall out of his hand at any moment. That scared the daylights out of me because even though he wasn't pointing the gun directly at me, I knew it was unstable and if dropped it could possibly go off. That I did see in movies. He opened the door all the way exposing me completely to his view and saw the puddle on the floor.

He closed the blue wooden, imperfect bathroom door all the way. There still wasn't a lock but there may as well have been with him now in and on the same side as I was. He started to make fun of me. He called me a big baby and a little bitch and said I was in even more trouble because I peed on the floor. Like I could help it?! I was shaking uncontrollably, still dripping and sitting in my urine and I couldn't look away from him. I guess I was so scared of that gun I couldn't take my eyes off him in fear of him actually shooting me??? What had I done to piss him off? Call me clueless because I was. He was definitely nipping at something because the closer he got to me I could smell his nasty breath. I knew it was some sort of alcohol, but I don't know what kind. He crouched down very close to me. He was still wearing his navy blue uniform which consisted of navy work pants and a navy work shirt. He had a name patch, white with navy lettering...*Jared* was right there and all who saw him knew his name but they had no idea that name patch should have read *evil*.

He proceeded to tell me that Mom was going to be really pissed that I peed behind the bathroom door on the floor. And how was he going to explain that??? Like he was going to tell her...it was the booze talking. I wasn't worried about that. I was however worried about the six shooter he still had in his hand. He was kind of tossing it back and forth from one hand to the other. Maybe it wasn't even loaded? That did not even occur to me at the time and I didn't want to take any chances. He grabbed me by my arm and slid me across the bathroom floor. He pulled me towards the middle of the bathroom and I found myself near the toilet. My head was vertical to the door and he forced me down on my back so I could lay lengthwise with the floor space. The bathroom was longer than it was wide. He squashed me down so hard I remember the nasty cracked and peeled back portion of the vinyl flooring pressing hard into my back. It was kind of curled up where it was cracked and split open…and it hurt! I was crying and my face was soaked like I had been out in a rain storm and my bottom half including my legs wet in urine. Good times right? What memories a child should have. Freaking sickening.

I saw him put the gun down near him. He squatted down once again and he started to take off his shirt, and then stood up and took off his pants and his not so "tidy whiteys". His blow gut hung over his underwear…he was repulsive. I loathed him. And he would repeat his stupid fuckin' so called jokes over and over and over…especially the one about his "blow gut". He would say "I have the Dunlap Disease… this is where my stomach dun laps over my belt!" HAHA…HAHA my ass! Fuckin' hated his STUPID jokes and he thought he was sooooo fuckin' clever and funny. Fuckin' dumb ass nasty redneck! He'd laugh at himself and after so many times of repeating these "jokes" people just started shaking their heads…no one laughed…it got old real quick! He was a total douche who thought he was all that…and a bag of chips. Well we all know those chips contributed to his "Dunlap Disease" now don't we.

So he stripped down to nakedness…grotesque…and I kept looking over at the gun…look at him…at the gun…and begged to him to please let me go. I assured him in my pleas that I wouldn't tell mommy…I wouldn't tell anyone…pretty much the usual for me. He was stern in pointing out that I was NOT going anywhere and he picked up the gun and put it to my temple. He went into that creepy voice reminding me that if I did tell anyone, especially my mom, that he would kill "them all" and kill me as well. Now I was fuckin' pissed and threw a hissy fit not caring if he did blow my head off…I even taunted him. Stupid, I know. But I was tired of being scared out of my mind constantly and being his little sex slave and punching bag whenever the mood struck him. I had enough in my mind at that moment and told him..."Go ahead shoot me! I want you to shoot me! Just do it! Get it over with! I can't take this anymore!" I was flailing around and I was struggling with him sitting on my legs and pinning me down at my shoulder with his *fuckin' bad ass gun* to my head. I found myself not giving two shits about his fucking gun and wanted it all to end. I was ready to die. I figured it was better than living like I was. I hated every aspect of my life and didn't care if I continued to breathe at that moment. He slapped me across the face and my nose started to bleed. I was gasping for air and choking. I could taste my own blood going down the back of my throat as he was not letting me up off the floor. I was shaking my head from side to side...lifting my head up but struggling, struggling like I never had before. He put his one arm across my chest up near my neck pinning me down HARD, and held the gun in his right hand to my head and said "Don'tchu fuck with me little girl! I'll fuckin' put your pretty little brains all over this bathroom!" Then I thought...ok...there's a good possibility he has bullets! I didn't say anything at first. I couldn't. I was still dealing with all the shit in my throat, bloody nose, snot, and more tears than a Lifetime movie. He reeked of what I now think was whiskey or bourbon and I knew he was probably serious and yet I still didn't care. I do remember telling him that he should go ahead and shoot me. I told him he would never get away with it and everyone would know what a pig he was. I told him I hated him and I wished HE was dead. I told him, yelling, that I didn't care anymore so just do it!!! He hit me in the head hard as hell...I don't know if it was with the gun or with his hand. It hurt so bad...and I don't remember anything after that.

He either knocked me out, or I blacked out. For how long...I don't know. What happened? What *did* he do to me? I'm not sure. I do know I had a bad, bad headache. None like I had ever had before. My head wasn't bleeding anywhere. I didn't feel a prominent lump. My hair was a little messed up, and that could have been from me

◄ "DON'T TELL MOMMY"

being that fish out of water. I still had blood on my face as I got up and looked in the bathroom mirror. I then noticed he wasn't in the bathroom with me any longer. Where was everyone else? I had no idea. I don't remember. I believe Jared came home early from work and found me alone there. So where was he now? I cleaned off my face and tip toed across and down the hall to my room. I was weepy and hurt everywhere...including "down there". I didn't think about anything but getting clothes on and hiding in my room in bed in hopes of Jared not returning to *bother* me again that late afternoon. I may have been home sick from school. I often had ear and throat infections growing up. But I don't remember. I can only speculate on that but if I had to guess that's what I was doing there when I normally would have been in school. My mom was working and my brothers and sister were at school.

So I was picking up my clothes Jared had basically ripped off me and I saw my shirt was ripped at a button hole, my panty's elastic was stretched out at the waist and both leg holes, and I didn't see my jeans anywhere at the time. I was tossing out quite a bit of undies for years. I guess my mother just figured I was messing myself and unsanitary because I was always in need of new ones. I remember needing to wear some of my sister's at times and I did not like doing that. I felt something running down my leg. I knew what it was without looking. So I looked and sure enough there was some of Jared's semen sliding down my thigh and there was some on my coochie area and I noticed something different this time. There was what seemed to be a little blood. I have said before I wasn't sure what happened when I was "out", and I don't know for how long. But I do know that in whatever amount of time it took Jared to get his evil juice out on me...he did it. How he did it is a mystery to me. I had hurt everywhere so I don't honestly know if he had achieved full penetration inside me or partial like he has in the past. I had always kicked and screamed...fought back and complained soooo much that the pain of him trying to enter me was so excruciating that he never got his disgusting penis inside of me or did he? But now, with this incident, I didn't know and am sick of the thought that he may have. I will probably never know if he full blown *raped* me. I was not sure if I was no longer a virgin at this point. I am horrified at the thought. I knew I was a victim of sexual abuse and molestation, but was I now a rape victim too?

Another incident occurred maybe a month or so after this one involving a knife. I know there was more than one with a knife but distinctly remember the first time he pulled one on me. I know it happened again in the bathroom and he had a pocket knife of sorts I guess or a hunting knife is probably the better term, but it could bend in half and the blade was probably as long as a grown man's fingers…maybe four inches or so. It had a brownish handle and was silver in color, probably stainless steel I am just guessing here. Maybe it was for fishing. He fished and hunted a lot so he had all kinds of shit he could use against me in the house and out in his black pickup truck. The truck also had a "cab" cover over the back so things could be stored in there out of sight as well as providing a hidden space from anyone's sight if he wanted to take me in the back and do his…well you know now basically what he made me do. So the only thing I really remember about this time was the knife to my throat…and for the life of me the rest is a blur. I was on my back face up on the floor…but only remember after the incident and him threatening to slit my throat.

I was standing naked in my room. Crying like a baby. I was looking for clean clothes to put on and I heard Jared say from the hall… "Katelyn"…real quick. He startled me. I turned around and he took a Polaroid of me, naked. What does this mean??? I will tell you a little later…be patient…it's worth it.

CHAPTER **11**

My Saving Graces ☺

AS THE YEARS dragged on, I may have become numb to some of the abuse or just repressed it. But as I grew, Jared still looked at me as a "child" and that I was, being under the age of eighteen the entire time I endured his abuse. I stated earlier in my tale of terror that I never had "good" friends until high school. I hid my emotions and carried myself like I was as normal as the next kid as best as I could. I must have been great at denial because I can't act or pretend for shit. But I got pretty good at pretending and thought maybe, just maybe Jared will stop. Stop making me live what I deemed to be hell on earth in that spooky looking house or on a windy back road in the infamous Pocono Mountains.

Not so fast…

High school began and I had established a couple of close friends. Again, as in the situation with Winnie, I would spend the majority of the time going to others' houses instead of them coming over to mine. You know the many reasons why. I got into cheerleading and found that I was pretty good at it. Back then it was nothing like it is today…far more conservative in dance. Love the acrobatics today… AMAZING athletes! Unfortunately today my opinion is that the dance aspects incorporated in cheerleading and the competitions are far too provocative and sexually suggestive. I personally feel there should be a "strip squad" instead of a cheer or dance squad because of just how explicit these moves are that young people display in public and get judged on. Since when did gyrating and twerking sit well with us and become cool??? And they start soooo young too! It shows you how lack of morals and decency has gone down the toilet in America today...and that's just one aspect and it's a damn shame! It seems the sluttier the moves the better they think they are...really??? Yikes! (That's my opinion and I'll tap into related issues misusing sex later and explain my opinions.)

So yes, let's talk about cheerleading back in the day. You may think it's trivial and long gone, but for me it played a huge part in keeping any sanity I may have had inside of me. These were the days where your precision and technical level of jumps and motions in the cheers for your team was the most important thing, as well as a genuine smile and not ridiculous flirtatious *winky faces*! I know times have changed. I still have opinions and I share them. OMG! Okay...I'll stop...LOL... But we were limited in how high pyramids could go, how revealing our uniforms were and believe it or not it became an issue of how much the girls with the bigger boobs would bounce...it is all true! It was the late 70s and early 80s now. But wow! We were asked NOT to wear T-shirts and our gym shorts at games while cheering because we tucked them in so no skin showed in the mid section...but they were banned because some of the girls' boobs bounced too much in the T-shirts!!! I kid you not! Anyway, our "dance routines" were more robotic and limited in provocative movement. I must tell you and send out a silly apology to two girls I was on JV Football Cheerleading with. We will call them Gidge Gosslinger and Mindy Masterson. They were very good dancers and had the sexier moves back then and I was the Captain of the squad and I was told to make them "tone it down" because coach thought they looked too sexy. They were awesome girls and grew to be fine women and I just hope they understood...I had to stay on them...I'm sure they were pissed way back when.I was probably called a bitch or a prude but that's how it was. I am pretty sure my overly conservative nature wasn't from nature at all. I am betting it derived from what I was going through at home with Jared. I knew it didn't help me do any *sexy* moves, that is for sure!

Moving on…cheerleading became my passion and a definite outlet for me to focus on rather than what I was enduring at home at the mercy of Jared. I knew there would be times when I would need some things from Jared for Cheerleading. Whether it may be some money for fees, an occasional ride out of desperation in not getting one from someone, anyone else, or him seeking me out during winter when the after school activity bus would bring me to my bus stop at 6;00 pm and it was already dark. I had to attend every practice, always. I had a choice. I took a chance. I knew he would find a way to get to me either way. I chose to do something that made me feel like I was somebody at least…I had the respect of my fellow cheerleaders because they voted me as their captain and I clung to that. Believe me, I needed that! I needed them…this bunch of intelligent, yet goofy girls, who would become my rock and not even know it. My *Saving Graces* as I now call them.

Still, no one questioned my home life. The other girls I cheered with just knew we were poor and they didn't pick at me for that. They did not make fun of our patchwork turquoise puttied Torino shit mobile. (The putty was for patching gaping rusted holes in the bodywork and the car had them everywhere!) It was old, hideous and the other vehicle we had at the time. All our cars and trucks were unreliable and embarrassing because they were so junky looking. It sucked when that wasn't common at my school. The Poconos was known more for the "ritzy"…aka…tacky, honeymoon resorts. Those resorts are gone today and there are casinos in their place. People that lived within the school district at Pocono Mountain Senior High School were usually housed in a nice development, or a subdivision, as they are called these days. The district zone was a wide spread area that spanned out for miles and miles. Nothing like smaller school zones today that are overcrowded and pretty much have a school for every subdivision. The school up there now is a series of branches...Pocono North, Pocono South, etc....huge campuses! You never really heard much about the poverty, poor ass shit holes. These unsightly places were usually tucked away in the woods off the beaten path and a dirt road. That's the category I fell into...and never got out of until my senior year.

I owe all those girls that befriended me a world of thanks for their acceptance and kindness. I was proud to call them friends. They were never mean to me, at least not to my face and if that happened, I am okay with that today! They treated me equally and helped me with rides and whatever else, sometimes money for a slice of pizza. They helped me if they could. I had one friend who was my *bestie*, we did not talk like that in the 80s...like - oh my God! LOL...I *must* share my memories of her and her unknowing wonderful impact she had on my life. We will call her Emma Laurville. She had dark hair and a big perfect smile and she was a total spazz! I loved hanging out with her! Emma was soooo perky you wanted to slap it out of her sometimes... for real! But she was key in sticking by me for many years and put up with some lying bullshit on my end and I can't say enough thanks to her for being there for me. She had no idea about my abuse, no one did, but she was always having me over to her gorgeous house. Her mom was funny as shit and had a crazy funny laugh that made me laugh...it was contagious. Emma had that kind of laugh too and it was awesome! I LOVED sending time at their house. It was on a beautiful lake in the woods. I thought they were rich! Well compared to my family I know they were rich in more than just material things. I think her mom was into radiology and I don't remember what her dad did but they divorced after a while. He was a nice man. Emma had a little sister, Valerie. She was quirky and funny. I liked her hanging out with us but Emma didn't. Annoying little sister syndrome happened there I suppose. I know my sister didn't want anything to do with me, but I believe that was different. They even took me on vacation with them to Florida during the summer before freshman year and I wished they were MY family! For the record I love my mom! I'm talking in reference way back then remember. They also took me to Maine one year too! We went to the LL Bean store. They were very preppy! If it wasn't for them, I would have NEVER gone anywhere! I worked as a maid at a honeymoon resort and babysat whenever I could to make my own money and saved for things my parents couldn't afford so I didn't have to beg for any if I could help it. I have worked since I was 12 years old. (I'm only 47, but I'm tired! Details of all the careers I've had and been successful in and my struggles as well will come later!)

See…my life wasn't *total* shit like you would expect. I like sharing the good along with the bad. It keeps giving me hope.

So, Emma lived her dream and married her high school sweetheart. She had a few kids, lived in I think it was Virginia or West Virginia, but sadly I think she ended up divorced. I lost touch and need to reconnect. I did thank her years ago when I started *sharing* my life's experiences with some people. I thought she was going to have a heart attack…I shocked the hell out of her with the news of my secret the whole time we spent as friends. She meant a lot to me and I needed her to know just how much I appreciated her. She could very easily have been a bitch like a lot of other girls in our school. That was a title held mainly by the older girls who walked the halls as if they owned them. But Emma chose to be my good friend and I still cherish the friendship she once gave me. I hope she is doing well these days. I miss Emma, and many others that have disappeared as life has carried us in different directions, miles apart. I also hope to someday be able to hit a class reunion with my husband and maybe my kids, who are grown now. I would LOVE to thank as many people as possible who have touched my heart and kept me going all those years ago…in person…finally, and with a true smile on my face. I never smiled. There's one picture I believe in our yearbook with a forced smile on my face. But there's still time and I have more faith now, more than ever!

MY SAVING GRACES

Then there were the "misfits" I call us. I felt I fit in there famously. We were a mish-mosh mixture of kids who just hung out together for shits and giggles. There was a girl, Rose, who had huge puffy lips and long frizzy hair to match. Another that hung out with her was a girl who was a Donny Osmond fanatic! She used to fib about silly things and stuff her bra with tissues I was told. Brittney was a pretty girl. So was Rose in her own way. She probably grew up gorgeous! I hung out at Brittney's house and she would invite others over and we were just goofy in pretending we were disco stars on stage, we had fun. I kind of got along with all different cliques. The jocks. For the most part, probably because of cheerleading or they may not have given me a second thought. There were the geeks, lots of us. Not all of them were geeky looking, but they had the brains! I was in honors classes as well so I did well in that circle. The "Vo-Tech Stoners"…well everyone just assumed they were stoners because a lot of them smoked cigarettes. I think it just took a couple of them to be seen doing that and reeking of the *herbal essence* and the stereotype was set…I didn't smoke back then. I just got to know some of them and they were laid back and cool…hhmmm…

They were actually the smart ones for learning a trade for free! …Will we never judge?

CHAPTER **12**

Will It Ever End?

UNFORTUNATELY MY STEPDAD had to ruin more parts of my school life and cheerleading for me. He always tried to make it hard for me to pay for fees and things that were required. He would make me beg. One particular time I needed money that I couldn't come up with in the fundraiser that was presented to supplement the fees for cheer camp. This was soooo exciting for me to go to something like this... it was like a dream to me! It may sound trivial to most of you but that is how dirt poor we were...we did NOTHING! We had NOTHING! So I had no choice and he treated me like a common whore in doing so. He literally made me take off my clothes, in a manner that at first was not acceptable to him. So he talked me through how I was to "strip" off my clothes for him. I was mortified and crying as usual and needed to do what he said or I had to forfeit my spot on the squad because cheer camp was mandatory. I NEEDED that freakin' money! I know people say money can't buy you happiness, but it sure as hell can keep you out of some bad situations! He had already taken my innocence and dignity a long time ago, but it always hurt just as badly as if it was the first time. I reluctantly did as he asked, the way he asked because he had control. He did and I knew it and it fuckin' sucked! He laid out money in a trail like a path across the floor and made me come over to where he was sitting on the bed where he instructed and watched me disrobe. He then told me to get down on the floor, on all fours…like a damn animal…like a dog. I kept pleading with him, "Please don't make me do this", not even knowing exactly what it was he was going to make me do. His hardened decency was nonexistent as always and he would not take no for an answer. If I wanted that money, and there was probably almost two hundred dollars there, (and that was a butt load of money to us!) if I wanted it I had to humiliate myself yet again to get it.

He told me I had to crawl across the floor on all fours and slowly and pick up the money as he watched me from behind…yes…naked. Did I mention that there is that visual thing I think most men have going on??? I knew so far back that men had the God given genetics to be pigs before I had pubic hair…scary…I know! So I started my revolting journey and I started grabbing what was mostly twenty dollar bills and gripping them in my clenched fists as hard as I could. I would stop and get up a little when I would pick up more and he made me stop. Fuck, I was doing it wrong. I had to put it back on the floor and start again but this time I was to stick my butt out and up in the air as far as I could get it without getting up off my knees or my hands. I was to drag myself slowly. Ugh…and there he was on the end corner of his and my mother's bed…stroking himself. He had whipped out that famous jar of Vaseline that never seemed to run out, he probably had cases of it stored somewhere on the property…gross! I would stop and look back at him and saw what he was doing and he kept saying "Go slower, stretch your legs apart more when you go"…so disgusting and he climaxed by the time I reached the other side. I swear to you he shot it at me like I was a target. He hit my one foot before I even had a chance to get up. It was an extremely humiliating experience and I still have issues with that incident as a grown woman of forty seven years. I scraped his *spooge* off my foot on the braided rug and hauled ass out of there as I held on to that money for dear life and grabbed my clothes running to my room. He then went about his day as if all things were just normal and okay, as always. The one hundred and eighty dollars was all mine now. I guess I kind of took one for the

"DON'T TELL MOMMY"

team as well that day.

He tarnished my love for cheerleading in another way as well. Our front porch on the old farm house was also wooden, also grey and distressed. It had I think two steps that led up to it or down to our front yard, however you want to look at it. It had a black wrought iron decorative rail across the front that connected the two support beams for the roof of the old covered porch. I was about five feet seven inches at this time and the level of this rail was just right to support me as I wanted to practice my jump skills for cheerleading. The porch boards were severely weathered and when I would jump up and down on it, it had a bit of a spring action so the boards were not going to break or crack because I was jumping on it repeatedly. I would grab the top of the rail and stand about a foot away from it and do my thing. I was a sophomore in high school and scored as one of the highest candidates for football cheerleading that year and was given the option to move up with the older girls on the varsity team or stay with my former squad on JV. I chose to stay with the girls who had become my friends and pledged them my loyalty. That dingy old porch allowed me to better myself and be one of the best cheerleaders in the entire school. I was so proud and happy to stay and lead with my friends. It was comfortable I guess. I felt like an outcast in many other ways all through school, one of those "misfits" so to speak. But cheering with the varsity meant the extreme possibility of rejection from the older "cool", popular girls who had money and nice cars...and of course the hot boyfriends. (Including the guy who would become my husband and father of my children ironically enough, more on that to come as well.) ...I just wanted to fit in somewhere.

Well Jared would see me or hear me jumping like a pogo stick on our front porch often. I practiced any chance I got. I was always looking to improve my skills and have awesome jumps. Having long legs helped there. So Jared came up with yet another creative way to make me hate him even more in his repulsive demands. He had approached me and caught me off guard once again. I got pulled into a situation where I found myself naked, as the usual protocol of this sick man. He then commanded me to lie at the bottom of my parents' bed. So then I did that down on my back as he instructed. (Yes, of course I was crying and pleading for him to let me go!) I was lying across the bottom of the bed, aligned with the foot of the bed. He reached down and pulled my hair. He yelled at me and said "I only want your legs sticking out from under the bed." I was like "HUH?!" What the frig is he talking about? He told me to slide the top of my body under the bed, (my head, my shoulders, etc.) and I did so after clearing a path for me to fit. My mom and Jared had all kinds of shit stuffed under the bed for storage I guess. It gave them quick access to this shit if they needed any of it. Otherwise, any other crap would be up in the haunting attic or down in the damp, eerie basement. There was shoes, vinyl albums, magazines, boxes of puzzles, some clothes, some rags, etc. All of which was dusty as hell and I did not want to stick my head and face under there! And I didn't know what the hell he was going to do with me like this. I was glad it seemed like he wasn't going to force me to perform oral sex on him though. (That was the worst for me. Gag and puke. Enough said.) So I rolled over on my back and just laid there. My legs were together as tight as I could get them. My hands were up against the metal springs that the mattress sat on. Those metal springs tended to be noisy at times too. It was cheap shit. I was afraid he was going to jump or something and squash me under there. I had no clue why I was in this position. It was a first. He told me to scoot down a little. I did. Then some more as he requested… exposing my coochie now and my belly a bit. Oh shit! WTF??? What is he doing? More important, what is he going to do? So he said then, "Now you like jumpin' up and down on my fuckin' porch so much, do what you do on the porch, I wanna see." I was like…what the hell is he asking me to do? I was totally confused…and scared. Weirdo! Nut case! Whack job…and now about to whack off I'm guessing. I tried to explain to him I didn't know what he meant. He replied, "I want you to open your legs like you jumpin' up n down makin' all that noise on my fuckin' porch!" Seriously? You want me to do what?

A jump...well a spread eagle as it was called...naked...and on my back. He didn't want to see my face, okay. I was stalling and with hesitation telling him that I still didn't understand. He was getting impatient with me and grew angry because I was taking too long. He literally took matters into his own hands. He told me to give him my feet. What??? "Kick your feet up here" he demanded. Crap, what's up with this? I thought. I was a little panic stricken at this point. I definitely didn't want a beating or another bloody nose. I got those way too easily and frequently. So up go my feet and of course my legs are connected. So there I am, under the bed. Legs up in the air, just great. OMG...I can't see a freakin' thing. He grabs hold of my ankles and smacks them together roughly. My bony ankles literally smacked together. I remember a pain shot up my legs. It didn't tickle.

He held me like that for a minute. He pulled back on them even more and made my butt lift off the floor. I was starting to fold in half which wasn't a problem for me. I was limber back then; well I can still bend over and touch the floor at least! I was fine but the bed was there... hello?! So now what? He takes my damn legs and pulls them apart... as far apart as his stubby arms would reach. Fuck! Yuck! And now I see, well I know what he is up to! God dang he is a filthy piece of work! Fuckin' pig wanted me to be on my back NOT showing my crying ass face, so he can watch my legs go apart then together, apart and together...what a mental fuckin' freak!

He is just soooo not right, in soooo many ways! Was he a product of being inbred? I will always wonder that. Was he himself sexually abused by *his* father? I witnessed good ole *Grand pop* getting a blow job from my sister once. Talk about burning a vision into your psyche!

Jared proceeded to force me to do this with my legs. I barely opened them and he got pissed and slapped my right thigh so hard that he left his hand marks in welts on my skin for hours. Hate him! He was pissy and no matter how far I did spread them he acted like it wasn't enough. He accused me of *faking* how far I could spread them. It was true. It was uncomfortable. It was mortifying. He knew how far I could open them while doing jumps and bitched at me to go wider. Then I heard that lovely sound of the Vaseline working its magic on his penis for him. His hands must have been going a mile a minute… ugh. He was staring and beating off to the sight of my vagina. I heard his moans once again. How disturbing.

CHAPTER **13**

Don't Mess With Mother Nature? I'll take My Chances... Crap...I'm Evolving!

I was now in high school and a teenager for some time. I had been blessed (more like cursed) with womanhood...my period, at the age of fifteen. That's late for girls these days but was an average age to start your menstrual cycle back then. At any rate Mother Nature hit me and I had developed the pubes and kind of missed the booby train, but that was okay with me. Considering I had a grown man groping me since I was six years old, I really didn't care or want big boobs at that point. Needless to say I was somewhat self conscious and shy about my body. Even though I became a "woman" officially by Mother Nature's standards, I was shy about my body. Duh, of course, right? I would crawl into shower stalls sometimes to change clothes for gym class. (Yes, P.E. now)

So my shy self had the bottom of the barrel everything when it came to clothes and yet another reason for me to hide. I hated it all...even my undies and little training bras. I was paranoid that other girls, especially the older ones, would look at me and say nasty, mean things about me and how I lacked any fashion wardrobe style. I felt like an eye sore. I wished I had a different life.

Once I started getting my period, I found out that my mother told Jared the news. My sister had already been having hers for more than a year longer than me. I didn't want it. I knew what it meant. It was gross and I felt so dirty. I would then use that dirty deed of my own to try to escape the torment Jared may have planned for me at times. That backfired. I lied a few times and wore the 2 x 4 pads between my legs just to try to fool him. When he would try to *mess with me* once I got my period I would cry wolf thinking I could possibly get out of his wicked grasp. It worked a couple of times but then I got caught. He called me out on it and actually checked me for blood. I freaked out and thought for sure he was on a new mission to try to get me pregnant. That was my worse fear. My period meant I was able to get knocked up by the devil himself. I can't imagine what some women have gone through, having been raped and given birth to the child of the demon who deposited their evil spawn inside them. How hard that would be for me. OMG to the millionth! I was always told sperm can travel even if the ejaculate is just inside the vagina. I believed it. I also feared the pre-ejaculate clear stuff...you know...the clear goop that sometimes leaks out. I believed that could get you pregnant too and that is why the pull out method was a bad idea as a form of birth control. I was fifteen. I couldn't go and ask my mother for birth control pills! How do I explain that? There wasn't a damn thing I could do and I believe to this day that *someone* was watching over me, somehow. And I WILL say Amen to that.

CHAPTER **14**

Meet The Fellas...

I HAD ONLY made out with a guy at that age, NO-Not my stepfather. Thank God he didn't make me do that. He tried to stick his tongue in my mouth when I was in middle school once. I bit his tongue so hard I tried to actually bite a piece of it off. He hit me so hard I saw into the next week! He never tried that again. Too bad I couldn't do that to his weapon of destruction...his penis. Lorena Bobbitt had the right idea! You go girl! Only my stepfather would find it up his ass, not in the woods. ☺

And now on to the good guys. First, his name was Adam Bobson. Not really, but you know you have to guess and figure out names and places all on your own! It happened...my first French kiss on our 8th grade field trip to Washington, D.C. He was a good kisser. He gave me the foundation to become an awesome kisser...or so I've been told... ;-) ;-)

He had kind of Stephen Tyler mouth...weird that's who popped in my head just now, I know! I never desired Stephen Tyler sexually... Lord that man is skinny! And that's a rule. I will have no man whose ass is smaller than mine, and I'm a size 4! He does have great teeth though...props to the man! Love the music...the smile is appealing... Sammy Hagar has another fav sexy smile! (Can you say ADHD?)

MEET THE FELLAS...

...Anyway...getting back on track...

But my very first smooch, just a peck, okay a longish peck, was in 6th grade with a chubby boy, not by much. I thought he was adorable. He was so nice to me and he was smart too. His name was...wait for it...You know it's not going to be his real name, but we will call him Stevie Bensen. We exchanged phone numbers and he was kind of my boyfriend, well I guess maybe only in my mind. I think at that point I was yearning for a "boyfriend" thinking it may force my stepfather to leave me alone and step off. Hah! It would have had to be Superman to keep that horny bastard away from me! I could dream. And I did. I had minor crushes here and there. There was another adorable boy. A slightly chubby blonde haired blue eyed boy in 7th grade. His name was Willie Billis. He and I clicked and became friends fast. We had all the same classes and I had a little crush. We never kissed, I don't think or I'd remember if was any good and I'm sure it would have been magical! Hmmm... And then one day he was just gone. He left the school as fast as he arrived. After about a week of his absence I asked my English teacher, who was also his homeroom teacher, "Do you know why Willie hasn't been in school all week?" She then told me he had moved back to Maryland or Massachusetts, or wherever he came from only months ago. I think his dad's job was the reason for his urgent departure and maybe it was difficult for him to call me and talk about it. I do know I was sad. There weren't really any other prospects for me to crush on. Even though Jared had plagued me with nothing but horrid experiences with him, I knew not all guys were like that. And I knew Jared was far from normal in any sense. Like I said... inbred??? I still had real feelings. I still had dreams of having a cute boyfriend someday. I found myself admiring physical features from afar and in the slightest company of members of the opposite sex. I was extremely shy. Interaction with guys was minimal and something I avoided heading into high school. There really wasn't anyone to really think twice about until 9th grade. ...Then one day holy crap!

This one hit me like a shot of flaming Sambucca!

CHAPTER **15**

Hubba Hubba!

I SWEAR WHEN I left 8th grade I was one of the tallest girls alongside my peers, guys included. Well I don't know how it's possible, but I went to the big high school now and remember walking down the hall on the way to homeroom that first day, I found myself constantly dropping my jaw at the guys who had also moved up into 9th grade! What the hell!? They were all at least a foot taller than I was! Okay, maybe not that much but I had to look up at most of them to talk to them or peek into their eyes in awe. "Wow!" I remember saying to my friends as we were admiring the view..."What the hell did their moms feed them over the summer...Miracle Grow???" I was blown away, excited, and also scared that these dweeby guys had metamorphosized into these hunky, kind of dreamy *stud muffins*! I'll never forget the first time I saw *him* that day. His name was *Tom Balco*. Most people called him Tommy. Yeah, whatever, not exact name! I hope he finds out this is about him because he NEEDS to know just how much of an impact he had on me way, way, back in the day. ☺

Tommy was an Italian guy who had the best head of jet black hair on a guy that I had ever seen! His hair was perfectly coiffed as it feathered back and shined. He had olive skin, dark sultry eyes, and a killer body of a true athlete. I am not sure I knew him in middle school, but I must have seen him in 8th grade somewhere because the first day back of 9th grade, he came towards me and my friends and BAM! (Middle School was a drag and I think I try to forget the bad stuff.) The first glance of him hit me like a hurricane named Katrina! Whew! As we passed each other in the hall we said a soft "Hey, what's up?" and a "How you doin'?" I probably needed a towel to wipe the drool of my mouth! I remember walking but looking up at him as he passed by. Or was I floating on air??? However, I know I was thinking "Damn! Hello beautiful!" I know I said shit to my friends like "Have you noticed how much these guys have grown over the summer?! How is that possible???" I was truly dumbfounded! I was amazed, excited, and a little bummed out. All these emotions and feelings, feelings like I had never had before, not until I saw Tommy that day. Physical feelings that said, "Katelyn, there is a God!" That was probably the first time I had actually felt like a *normal girl* in my life. All thoughts of home went out the door. (Or should I say…down the hall?) I was overwhelmed with what my eyes were privileged to see that first day back, and I thought for a while that it was going to be a good year. Honestly, it didn't take long for my enlightenment to hop back into reality as by the end of the walk to homeroom, I also saw how freakin' awesome a lot of the girls looked too. Now as a forty something woman, I am happy to say that I am more secure with myself in comparison to being that awkward, skinny, bland, hick from the sticks, who knew she was *not* a top contender in the world of new *freshman hottties*. I never thought I was attractive. I never thought of myself as an interesting person to talk to. I used humor to mask all that I was hiding inside. I never made myself available for anyone to get *too close* to me. I was afraid of what they may find out. So that fleeting moment of joy had fizzled fairly quick as I realized once again that my life sucked. The girls had nice new clothes. Most had new Calvin Klein jeans like Brooke Shields, and the butts to fill them. I had maybe two new pairs of pants that year and one new pair of shoes, deck shoes…no Jimmy Choos by far…and I bought whatever I did have by myself. I had to. I hated getting dressed for school each morning. It was depressing. I did however have one thing. It was the jealousy of just about every other girl I knew. Even if their styles were different I knew it was at the very least nice. For example, one was preppy and another dressed like a biker chick, but they still had the cool new stylish clothes, boots, shoes, and purses. They had all the accessories and jewelry to pull it all off and catch the eye of any guy that would sneak a glance at them. Okay sneak is putting it politely. Teenage boys hitting serious puberty...they were gawking at girls and all their body parts! I knew, or at least thought that very few guys looked my way. I was along for the ride most of the time you could say, as the guys checked out my friends. I wasn't stupid. I knew they were not really looking at me. All I really had going for me was cheerleading and I had brains. Like I said before, if it weren't for cheerleading I probably could have gone through high school without anyone really noticing I was there.

Now I have so many pretty girls in our school that I have to look at every day. I would now wonder what it would be like to have beautiful clothes, flowing hair, nice cars, a nice home, and dream of a cute guy of my own to kiss outside class each day. That was a big thing in high school. PDA...public display of affection. Some couples would be tongue wrestling and the teachers would have to pry them apart to force them to get to class. Some would walk hand in hand. Some would be hanging on each other so bad, groping each other's body parts so much that they would be told to knock it off and get a room already! It was nauseating and sometimes even a bit of a freak show, but it didn't stop me from wishing I would someday have someone to have the *hots* for me like that. And of course I longed for Tommy. He was a dream. Ahhhhhhh. I knew he was way out of my league.

I would get made fun of from time to time about my wardrobe and cry like crazy. Sometimes I would run to the bathroom crying and risk getting detention because I was late to class because someone was bullying me. It was both guys and girls. Kids are cruel today and they were long ago as well. Mean people suck. And in the chance to thank all those who were kind and accepting to me, I would *also* like the chance to confront those who were douche bags to me as well. Maybe someday. Judging me on how I was dressed or how parts of my body looked…what kind of car my parents had. The hurtful comments and teasing lasted until I was a senior in high school. I don't know how I got through it. Oh…that's right I do. His name was Tommy.

Tommy was one of the most sought after hunks in high school history, well I thought so, and he did have a little bit of a reputation of being a "dumb jock". Yikes! I hate saying that, but some girls that would go out with him would say things making him sound like he was a dumb ass. Maybe he was. I didn't have many classes with him. I was in the advanced ones. He may have had some too and we had different teachers and schedules, I don't know. But did I care??? Hell no! Not at that point. Nothing anyone could say would tarnish the God-like guy I now lusted after, *in secret* of course!

I never really spoke of my HUGE crush on Tommy with anyone because I knew I was dreaming and would look stupid if they knew. Word spread fast up there in those mountains! (I definitely don't miss that!) So I kept my feelings to myself and just went along with the notion that a lot of the male *"newbies to puberty"* in the 9th grade were brainless, horny, and even sometimes pimple covered dudes. Yep, I said dudes. It was 1980! I still wanted Tommy.

I would become friends with those guys on the teams I cheered for. Again, probably just because I was a cheerleader. At least I looked better in my uniforms than my regular crappy clothes! So during bus rides to and from games or in classes I would talk a little with some of the guys I felt were somewhat approachable. I became really good friends with one black guy at our school who was basically the star of the football team. (We were a predominately white/rich or redneck school. There were only a handful of blacks in our school back then.) His name was Tom too. He had a younger sister who I thought was the funniest girl I had ever met… with a voice and awesome personality that always made me laugh! She was very pretty too. Her name was Lacey. So me being friends with our own mini version of Bo Jackson you could say, I was worthy of some additional conversations with more and more of the guys from time to time. I was okay with that. I also took some ribbing and actually called a "nigger lover", yep, I said it, because it happened, one of the dumb ass jocks said it. I'll never forget how word of that flew through the school and this guy almost got the shit beat out of him. (And it would have been well deserved.) He has since as an adult become a distant friend that I need to reconnect with. He lives in Jersey with a nice family and he really isn't racist. His name was Don. Don was a good friend of Tommy, my crush too. I think he did that back then to choose and find a reason to be mean to me…and he chose poorly. I know he didn't *truly* mean it. We all make mistakes. However now, it was bad enough my stepfather *was* racist as hell and made comments about my friendship with the black kids. I'm not referring to them as "African Americans" because we just said *black people* back then. I mean no disrespect and wanted to be clear on that. In fact I knew Tom and Lacey so well that if you were to walk up to them and refer to them as politically correct, African American, they would have busted out laughing in your face! They were that cool and not uptight about their skin color. They never used it as a crutch! They were proud of their heritage and earned the respect of most whom didn't see them for their skin color. They would have said something like…"You mean my black ass?!"…and be laughing! You disrespect them, and then you deserve what you get. Just like anyone in this country expects…know what I mean??? People still need to relax and see past the damn color of skin. That word to me is a form of behavior…in *all of us*…*in any color*… that needs to be the focus! Stupid controversy and shame on us all for misusing words and giving them extreme value when they are but that…words. Our behaviors is what is important…NOT our skin color…for goodness sake already! Look what the fuckin' white guy was doing! (I get so pissed.) **Evil is evil**…it does not discriminate…and it will *always* come in many shapes, forms, sizes, genders, and colors. That's my opinion and if you don't like it...tough shit. Let's move on.

Back on track again...

So either Lacey or her brother Tom would spend a lot of time with me on the phone at night. We lived our teen years in the days of some rotary dial phones with curly cords. We even had a *party* line where we had to share, yes share our phone service with someone else in the area. If the call was for our house it would ring twice in short rings. If it was the call was for the other house it would ring once and it would be a long ring. That is how we had phones back then. Can we all LOL now about that Stone Age we called the 80s?! So good ole daddy dearest got tired of me associating with the black kids and talking on the phone so much that he actually put a fuckin' lock on the phone! The dial was actually able to have this little lock that slid on it. Can you say *control freak?* Only he and my mother had a key. I remained friends with Tom and Lacey, but Jared made it difficult for me to have any form of social life, as you can see. White, black, it didn't matter. It was just guys especially. Funny thing, he didn't mind if I was friends with girls, not so much fuss there. Hhmmmmm. I am guessing you know why I say that there!

There was a time when I had a friend Donna who had a bit of a reputation of being a, how do I put it delicately...well there is no way... so I'll just come out and say it...slut...in school. It is what it is people. I didn't judge her for being "friendly" with a lot of guys and I guess she didn't judge me for being...well...me. She had a little brother the size of Shaquille O'Neal and they lived in Pocono Summit. She was more experienced in everything compared to me. She seemed to know a lot about sex, smoking, partying, and all the fun stuff! It was high school and by this time I was a junior and in my eyes and between my legs I considered myself to be a virgin. Even though I wasn't sure if Jared took that from me or not, I never really had any serious social encounters with other guys. I hadn't really done anything more than kissing and maybe a little rubbing around outside

"DON'T TELL MOMMY"

the clothes. One stupid ignorant jack ass even made fun of me after a date because I was so shy and conservative. He made fun of me because he said I didn't know how to give hickeys! He said I was inexperienced because I wouldn't let him grope me. If he had only known I had already been through things that are seen in porn movies. Ick! He was an asshole and didn't deserve my attention in the first place obviously! Jerk off...he thought he was so cool. His name was Denny. Ooooh...he was in a band. He played the drums. BFD. Did he ever think maybe that was all his hands were good for? Needless to say, Denny was *not* hickey worthy.

So Donna came over to my house for a sleepover one night. I remember she was wearing her boyfriend at the moment's football jersey and her bikini underwear. And that was it. That's what she would sleep in. The jersey barely covered her ass and the top bagged out where you could see her boobs if she bent over. (Well the jersey was meant to go over football shoulder pads, so yeah it was big.) She thought it was cool and so did I. But I thought you should wear your guy's jersey over a turtle neck along with jeans at school. Not to serve as a nightie with my ass hanging out at my friend's house. I had brothers too. Ya' think she liked attention? That's a big affirmative!

My stepdad was not around and I think he was supposed to be gone until late but he was there before we went to bed. We would dance around up in my room, my sister went somewhere doing God knows what. Donna was a good dancer. She wasn't afraid to shake it I guess. Jared came upstairs and quickly opened my door without knocking. He saw Donna in her sleeping attire and didn't even look my way. I had a warm shirt and sweat pants with socks on. I was always cold. I remember this gross grin coming across his ugly face. He said "I was wonderin' what all the commotion was about up here!" I thought for sure he was going to raise hell with me and be pissed off. We were loud and the jumping up and down from the beds to the floor making a ton of noise! Nope. Nothing! He just stood there for another minute and then said tone it down some and then he closed the door behind him. Was he out drinking and came home in a good mood? Whatever the reason I was fine with not getting into falsely accused trouble for once. What happened next is something I don't quite understand. I remember I didn't think anything was wrong but I do remember Donna's mom showing up early the next morning. I guess to pick her up sooner than we had planned. She was flipping out once she came into the house. Parents rarely came into our house, like they would fear catching a disease or something…or maybe they were just lazy. I don't really know. Yet very few let their kid stay over once in a blue moon. Well that's about to come to a screeching hault!

I remember it was early morning and I was still upstairs and Donna had gone down to go home because her mom had arrived and I heard yelling from everyone when I was still up in my room with the door closed. I was like WTF? Donna's mom was yelling at my stepfather and accusing him of trying to *touch* her daughter the night before. Apparently Donna called her mom early in the morning to come and get her as soon as possible! And her house was far too. A good thirty minutes between our houses if not longer. She was upset and said Jared came in my room late last night and tried to kiss her while she was in my sister's bed sleeping. I was like…WTF? Where the hell was I??? What the blazes was going on?! My mom said she didn't believe it and that Donna was making it up and probably wanted Jared to make a move on her. My mother saw how we were dressed when she came home from work. She obviously didn't approve of what Donna was wearing either and knew of her promiscuous reputation. I, on the other hand, was like…"Oh shit!" Donna didn't say anything to me. Why not? Why didn't she wake me when he was in my room after her??? I didn't like how she was dressed either but that doesn't give *any* man an excuse or permission to make any type of sexual advance towards someone who is not consenting…and especially a minor!

Oh my gosh! I knew Donna was probably not making it up…look at what all Jared had done to me! But no one else knew that! I don't know why but no one questioned me either after that incident. Had

"DON'T TELL MOMMY"

I wished that they did? I have always had mixed emotions about that question that I had asked myself from time to time. Would all hell have broken loose and Jared may have gone on a psycho killing spree for real if I chimed in??? I saw how my mom reacted to Donna's *news* and I knew if she had known what Jared had been doing to me...or to my sister...and possibly even my brother Todd...for all these years... whoa! I know she wouldn't have been able to handle all that for sure! My mom had high blood pressure and was on some serious medication for it. She was always anxious, like me, and got upset very easily. The kind of upset where she worries about the smallest damn thing compared to what a *normal* person may compare it to. She will worry months in advance about something and have her ass in a tizzy forever over it! It is insane! Handle that her husband was a fuckin' pedophile??? For all these years and she didn't know about it...oh hell no!

I knew by her reaction about Donna's incident over an attempted kiss that she would go over the edge and have freakin' heart failure if she knew the truth. I couldn't do that to her. What would become of all of us? I hated my life, but it was not just my life that would be affected. I was screwed. (I do not mean it literally either.L) And I kept silent in fear.

I did still hang out with Donna after that incident at my house with Jared, just not at my house. She was no longer allowed to come there...and rightfully so. Despite what had happened she was a friend of mine for a few years. We never really talked about it as far as I can remember, and that is sort of strange thinking back on it. But it's possible we did and I may have blocked that out because I probably would have been in a panic situation if we did. I don't know. I am thankful nothing worse happened and I am sorry for her that Jared had even attempted such a brazen thing with one of my friends. I honestly didn't think he would be stupid enough to try anything with someone outside our family. Oh...little did I know at the time. Oh... what you will learn later!

I took advantage of the generous opportunities given to me to be away from home. I did so even if the person who passed on the invite had some issues of their own. Who was I to judge? I knew of the skeletons in my closet that is for sure! I learned from some of my friends who had already lost their virginities that sex was a little scary the first time for them but it was well worth the second time, and so on. I learned the guys our age or around our age didn't know all that much about what they were doing. I am guessing girls shouldn't know all that much either. Some of the other girls explained to me how the male egos were over inflated and the guys thought they were so good at sex, but in reality they didn't really know how to *please* a female at that age. So kids experiment like I am sure they do today…oh that's right…there's the internet these days! But back then, I guess, is why God gave us all hormones and we had to practice, and learn, get educated as time goes on…learn by trial and error on how to become good lovers.

I had only dreamed about being intimate with a guy then. Jared had ruined my drive to pursue a male close to my own age. I had absolutely NO confidence in myself and I am pretty sure that was apparent to those who knew I existed. I think I may have been a bit of a mystery to most. I had noticed some of the guys were a little nicer to me than others. And this would usually happen when no one else was around. It may have been in study hall in an auditorium. It was in passing in the halls during classes when the halls were void of students and a task had to be completed. Tasks such as using the restroom, going to the library, or running an errand for the teacher. I realized some guys wanted to like me maybe…but they would be embarrassed to make that known to other people? That was how I was truly beginning to see how the opposite sex viewed me. An *okay looking* girl at best, who was intelligent but was popular due to the company she kept and the school activities she stayed involved in. Maybe they saw me as a diamond in the rough?

I clean up okay. The same as almost any person when they are given the right tools. Look at the women on television or in movies and in all the magazines today. It is pretty well known that you do not see anyone in their rawest, unaltered form *usually* because they are just as homely looking as most of the rest of us. There are exceptions. There are natural beauties, but ANYONE can look like a model with the right hair and makeup. Some have braved the decision to be photographed or filmed naturally and kudos to them! Like Cameron Diaz and Jamie Lee Curtis…you rock ladies! That's an unfortunate fact. It puts such unfair pressures and expectations on average people who live real lives in believing that men will only want us if we look *perfect!* Boo and shame on the advertising world! I look at magazines today or see someone online and think, "Wow…she is gorgeous! I wished I looked like her!" Well it took a long time, but I did realize that what we see is superficial and not the real way they look. They images are soooo altered, some so much they must look like a completely different person after a shower! And that is how I came to grips later in life about my looks. I accepted what I was given. I learned to be thankful with what genetics I had. It could have been worse, and actually, my appearance got better with age for me. Confidence can do that I learned. I no longer *wish* to look like someone else. I can only embellish and enhance a touch of what I have…and embrace it. If I wear spanx or padded push up bras all the time…that shit has to come off sometime and what is real is always going to be there. So why try to impress so badly? I have a husband who loves me for who I am and what I look like AT MY ABSOLUTE WORST! (Supposedly… is he a saint???) If so, I am either blessed or he is a great liar! So I don't do that shit. That's too much work…that's too uncomfortable. If someone doesn't like me they way I look when I am out and about… they can go fuck themselves. I am not here to worry about pleasing their vision of me. If I look in the mirror and can deal with myself and my husband is happy…that is all that matters. I wished I had just a little smidge of the confidence I possess today back in high school. I know when you are told certain things over and over and over again, you begin to believe them. You lose your own sense of self. You can't let that happen!!!

I got an unexpected boost one day that would end up changing my life at that point more than I could have ever imagined.

I am pretty sure it started in a study hall that I luckily shared with my ultimate crush, Tommy. It was my junior year and Tommy and I would be bored and become a little flirtatious, as he was known to be with many girls at school. I still felt special that he even looked my way! Well the note passing turned into a little proposition. How this happened, I couldn't tell you. But I *will* be happy to tell you all about how that smokin' shot of Sambucca captivated my heart.

CHAPTER **16**

My Own Endless Love

TOMMY WAS BY far the guy who was on my mind most of the time! He had been since freshman year. I was his secret admirer and now someone else he had full permission to flirt with. So what was in those notes we passed in study hall you may be wondering??? I hope you are wondering! Well I am happy to say Tommy actually asked *me* to meet *him* the next period by our lockers! I was like...Oh my God!!! Was I reading the note right??? Was I imagining what had been written on a simple piece of notebook paper, folded and unfolded many times? Nope. It was real alright! I remember looking up at him in the sectioned off auditorium with stacked seating, (I was in the row below him and a seat over. We had to scatter ourselves during study hall. It was a rule.) So I slowly turned my shoulder and head to look up at him and he was smiling! And what a great, perfect smile he had! Soooo sexy! I love great teeth! It says something about someone, I think so anyway. I take pride in my straightened pearly whites today and I smile! Something I never did growing up, so I admire and applaud those who take pride in oral hygiene!

So I just glanced at him like...are you for real?! You want *me* to meet *you...alone...*by our lockers??? Our lockers were located on the second floor of the school on and end hall, near a stair case. It was quiet and fairly private when it wasn't in between class rush time. Our lockers were tucked away along the back wall. It would be easy to be out of sight there. I had never thought of that until that day. I wrote back "How?" in the note I slipped back to him. He said to ask to use the restroom or go to the library...make up some excuse to get out of class and meet him at our lockers at a specific time. I replied okay. I asked what time am I to do this and he set a time. I was certainly feeling my heart pounding out of my chest. My pulse was racing! Whew! I was excited! Study hall was over and he started walking up the stairs and out the auditorium to his next class as I started walking down the stairs to go to mine. We kept looking at each other. He kept pointing to my hand at the note. A note I surely held on to for dear life. He was shaking his head and pointing nonchalantly, reassuring me he was serious. I was smiling and giggling like the school girl with a crush that I was...shaking my head in disbelief. I was now shaking all over as if I had a constant chill in my bones at this point and don't know how the hell I had even made it to my next class! But I did. I think I had English. I remember feeling that note in my pocket and keeping it tucked oh so tightly so I wouldn't be as careless as to lose it in the halls of PMHS. (Pocono Mountain High School) I kept looking at the clock. I was elated but also had a thought shoot into my head. One that I wasn't so excited about and dreaded that it could actually be true. It was the thought of Tommy totally pulling my leg and playing a cruel joke on me. Would he not show up and then tell everyone what he did and I would be laughed at for...well probably the rest of my high school life? Or would he send some other guys thought to be gross or loaded with acne or something in his place and play us both for fools? Or, could he show up with one or more of the muscle head goons and they mess with me only to laugh like hell later??? Yikes! I wasn't sure what to think. Was I thinking too much??? Was paranoia setting in??? After all, the only encounters I had dealt up until then was with the demonic dip shit I had to call daddy.

A feeling of oppression came over me as if the life was draining out of me right there in English class. The time had come and I would have five minutes to make it to my destination and rendezvous with Tommy. But was it real or just fantasy? Because I had wished for it so badly doesn't mean it will come true. If it were only that easy, right? Aren't our prayers supposed to do the same thing? We pray in hopes to our God to make the bad things go away in our lives. I knew my prayers had never been answered because my abuse was still a certain reality in my life. Why would I even begin to believe a simple wish would come true? For me...a nobody. Someone who had lost faith, someone who had no self esteem, someone who was dirt poor...and it was obvious by the way because they always seemed to smile with ease. I could never even smile in any true delight when everyone around me seemed to be happy. Why would something all of the sudden, be good for *me*? That oppressed feeling came and stuck with me as I wondered and already felt embarrassed before anything had even happened. Even the thought of Tommy actually being serious about this so called proposition now made me feel stupid. ... Like a child who had been cruelly tricked into wanting chocolate cupcakes so badly, that it changed her life forever.

I couldn't go. I just couldn't do it. I had myself convinced that Tommy was only playing me for a foolish girl in awe of him. He had to have known how I felt about him. He obviously caught me looking at him every now and again. I flirted with him if he initiated it. I took what I could from that and cherished it. Now...I didn't know what to do with it. It was tainted in my mind. Was he an asshole like Jared??? Ugh...were all guys like my stepfather? Is that even possible? Or... just maybe...my crush *wasn't* a total douche bag. The time had come to leave class. The bell sounded and everyone piled out into the halls. It was the last class of the day and everyone hauled ass to their lockers to get the hell out of school as quickly as possible. That was usual at the end of the school day. Even those of us who had an activity to go to practice rushed so we were not to be late.

I remember looking around as I walked and had meaningless conversation with a fellow cheerleader and classmate. I kept looking for

Tommy as I would typically see him behind me in the hall after the last class of the day or because his class was around the corner from mine on the other side of the building. I would usually take my time *just a little* sometimes so I may *accidently* bump into him or come out behind him to watch his ass while he drudged down the hall to our lockers. Funny though…he did walk a *little* like a Neanderthal! Ha! I didn't care! He had to have some flaws didn't he? I am sure his walk reflected his height and size…those growth spurts! I guess puberty was awkward for all of us!

So anyway, I couldn't see him anywhere. There were too many kids and too many people taller than me. I was actually hoping to NOT see him at that time. I'll be honest…as I always am…I was scared! Scared he had told one of those ass bag friends of his, what he had done. How he lured me to the lockers. How he now, for sure, knew I liked him so much. Fuck. Now what? I was at my locker finally. I started gathering my books and put together my cheer practice clothes in a bag and was getting ready to go to practice. I still didn't see him. The rest of my peers had pretty much filtered out and the locker area and halls became more and more quiet. There were only a few of us still struggling to get organized and head down the stairway.

Then out of nowhere…there he was! Shit! I looked to my right ever so slightly and he casually looked over at me. He was alone. I looked down and got the rest of my crap together but started fumbling like there was a bus I had to catch. Nope…no bus today. I had practice and he knew it. I got my things gathered up in my arms as best as I could and as fast as I could. Neither one of us said a word. In a flash he approached me at my locker before I was able to escape my humiliation. Aww fuck. This is just great, I thought. I needed to be invisible. I thought I was about to cry. He touched my shoulder and said, "Hey, where were you? Why didn't you come? Couldn't you get out of class?" I about shit my pants eight ways to Sunday! I replied with relief, "No, there was already someone out with the hall pass and they took forever. I figured you were gone." OMG!!! Was this really happening??? He asked, "Well maybe tomorrow?" I replied "Yeah, we can try again tomorrow. Sure." He said "Gotta' get to practice...see you tomorrow." "Yeah, see ya'." I think my voice was quivering when I squeaked that out to him. Wow. Like...really! WOW!!! What does this mean?!? Crap. Shit balls! Now I am instantly a train wreck about the possibilities that were put upon me...and I was really excited... and seriously scared!!!

I had to go to practice. How could I function when I could barely breathe now? I think I was in a catatonic state of shock because girls like me don't have guys like him propositioning them for a rendezvous at school. To quote Julia Roberts in Pretty Woman..."It was a great offer for a girl like me." And I knew it and I was in lala land and could not believe what had just transpired. I was relieved that he wasn't just another sick prick looking to bully me with his friends. I was overjoyed with the thought of him liking me at all! And now he wanted to do what? I didn't know!!! I was at practice and worthless. I think we practiced our dance routine for Friday's pep rally the entire time. Going through the motions was easy in memory and didn't require me to focus on any technical crap at that point and I had more important thoughts to focus on for the night. I had the other girls take turns watching us and critiquing our performance. They liked practicing our routine the most. Practice ended and I floated all the way home...on cloud 9, on 10, and I think there may have even been an 11!

CHAPTER **17**

Can I Pull Of Being *Normal*?

I WENT HOME that night after cheer practice feeling like I was the luckiest girl on the planet. I felt bad because I accused Tommy of being a pig like my stepdad without any true reason, which wasn't fair to him, and I felt ashamed of myself for doing so. I understand why my mind went there but I was not happy that it had gone automatically *there*. The shame on me became shame on Jared. Shame on him for making me doubt the one guy I had idolized in my mind. I allowed Jared's behavior to tarnish my opinion of Tommy. I knew I had some thinking…some daydreaming…some serious grooming possibly, (because I was now more paranoid!) and I had the night to dream of what may become at the lockers sometime tomorrow.

It wasn't long before I had gone from my *happy place*… (this is the place where my life is perfect and I have no stepfather…I have lots of money…where the free lunch program no longer applied to me for the first time in my school history…I am also gorgeous…and I have the guy of my dreams interested in me…Tommy!)…I went from my happy place, to a state of frenzy sifting through my clothes trying to figure out what the hell I was going to wear to school the next day! This was crucial! Probably the most important decision of my life up until then!

*LOL…I seriously thought that! Looking back as I write about my life, I have to laugh at myself and chuckle about how I reacted to some situations because they seem a little silly and a bit trivial now, only because I am grown and don't weigh material things the same as I did long ago. Then…it was the world to me! (I just needed to share that. Keeping my sanity people!)

So I had some serious finagling to do with very little in my selection of items I had to choose from. My mission was to "wow" my crush in the morning. I didn't want to blow the chance to meet him again. I wasn't going to give him the chance to change his mind. I ended up wearing my neatest, least worn, pair of pants. They were burgundy Lee pants that had an almost velour texture to them, almost like velvet. LMAO…I know! But they were actually in style…it was 1983! I chose a striped ¾ length sleeve shirt with a priest's collar, (that's the only way I know how to describe the collar). The colors were burgundy and white. It was a button down blouse and it had ruffles, big ones down the front! I can see my outfit clear as day!!! …And yet I can't remember if I put underwear on this morning!!! LMAO here. I also had burgundy leather deck shoes that were Etienne Aigner. I think that's how you spell the designer's name. I felt this was the best I had, and my butt, what little I had back there in that department, my tiny heiny looked best in these pants. I worked a lot of babysitting hours to buy that *amazing* outfit that I was so proud of. Tee hee…chuckling…you had to see it! Ah…the ruffles! So big! …

It was the 80s! I had some work to do. Would I get ANY sleep that night?

I am so thankful that someone was watching over me that night and kept my stepdad busy, and kept him away from me. I really needed to forget about him, even if it was for just a little while. I had gone to bed and was now picturing in my head the vision of Tommy being next to me. Standing with me in his arms and looking deep into my eyes, and kissing me like I was the only girl for him. I remember I practiced kissing on my hand! Yep! I'll admit it right now! Ha! I make myself laugh! I did what they show geeks doing on TV…I practiced making out…

on my hand! I had French kissed before, but not in a while! I was nervous about meeting Tommy at the lockers. We never discussed what we would be doing at the lockers, but I wanted to be prepared! Haha…so I made out with my hands while listening to Lionel Richie and Diana Ross singing Endless Love on my little 45 record player… over and over. I kid you not! Pretty sad, I know! Funny to me now! Forever in my memory…just like the next day.

The ride to school on the bus for me was typically 45 minutes… big school district, like I told you. It felt like hours went by before we would finally get there! Would I be happy or humiliated when I would finally get there?

CHAPTER **18**

Best Day...Worst Day Ever

I PRIMPED AND nervously squirmed about in my seat on the bus in which I occupied alone. It felt like forever but we finally arrived! I think I was so nervous that I could have peed my pants! I felt like I looked pretty good. Well, as good as I could get anyway. I couldn't sleep that night before as I found myself daydreaming instead of in a deep slumber dreaming of Tommy. That morning before the long ass bus trek I had spent extra time on my hair. Curling my poker straight hair was a chore and a half. It was shorter and I liked it to feather back. That was a popular style...remember...It was the 80s! Lots of hairspray while curling...the sizzle of it on the curling iron let me know I was going to be successful in my style. I would then lift and spray...and lift and spray some more. I was dressed in my best outfit, (haha) I did my hair, and had on a little makeup. Just some eyeliner and mascara. I never really learned how to do makeup all that well, so I always kept it minimal. I was sure not to forget my Bonne Bell lip gloss. I had a couple different flavors and that day I thought cherry would be quite suitable. Most of that brand's flavors are still yummy! I am obsessed with different lip balms and glosses as a grown woman. I have pouty lips which I was always subconscious about. People ask me now if I had collagen put in my lips...I am so happy to say NO! I've seen some scary plumping gone bad! Damn! Lumpy and distorted...lookin' all freaky! Who'd want to kiss that shit! So it wasn't until college that I learned to embrace my full lips. I was told that I was a great kisser…and I owe it to my pouty lips! Yippee for me, right? Hey…at least it's something!

I was on my way up to my locker. My eyes were peeled and looking for my secret crush. It wasn't until I went up the rounded stairwell that I arrived at my locker. There he was. He had his locker open, his books in his arm and he was talking to Don. Ugh…I hated being around Don back then…sorry Don! He was such a dick. He knows that's the past. So Tommy and Don finish their conversation. I was unsuccessfully opening my combination lock on my locker. I was so nervous and I just kept spinning the knob and missing my correct numbers. I was flustered and saw Tommy coming at me out of the corner of my eye. He walked up to me and said "Hey." I looked at him and said "Hi." My locker was still closed. We just looked at each other for a moment in silence and then he slipped me another note. I clenched the note, hiding it in my hand. I could tell he didn't want anyone to see him giving me that note. And I was okay with that. I was still just hoping and praying he was for real. I'm such a chicken shit! I know!

He smiled at me and said "Ya' think you can be here this time?" I replied "Sure. I'll make sure I'm here." He turned to walk away and said "See ya!" I said "Yes Tommy!" as he hustled to class as the bell for homeroom was now going off. Crap! I was late. That was okay because I had a hot little note in my hand and I couldn't wait to read it!

I got my books and got into homeroom and the teacher wasn't even in the room. I sat down threw my books on my desk and I slowly and carefully opened the note from Tommy, careful not to draw attention to myself. It was short and sweet in more ways that the cliché could ever mean. It simply read "12;45…show up this time!" His writing wasn't the best but I could read it clear as day. I had a social studies class during that time and the teacher was pretty laid back so I knew I could make up some excuse up to leave. I had lunch before that and was so nervous that I couldn't dare eat. I sat in the commons area instead and spent a lot of time in the girls' bathroom primping, knowing during the next class period, I was going to meet Tommy at our lockers. I was chewing gum and wanted to keep my breath as fresh as I could just in case. Just in case Tommy wanted to kiss me at our lockers??? Was that too crazy for me to think he would even want to? Yes, it was crazy! But I was still hoping and I had no idea of what to expect. It all could still backfire in my face and traumatize me if he was playing me for a dip shit. But I sure as hell put myself out there. I found strength from somewhere to take that plunge! Maybe it was in the way he looked at me so sweetly that morning. He made me feel that he wasn't capable of being mean to me like some of his ass bag friends. So the time had arrived. It was 12;40 and I was working on class work, some worksheet. I put on some Bonne Bell…just in case…and I got up and asked my male teacher if I could use the restroom. I had a sense of urgency in my voice so he would know I really HAD to go. The male teachers asked fewer questions when girls asked to use the restroom. They usually knew we had *female* issues to take care of sometimes. He handed me a hall pass without saying a word and away I went. Would I return feeling like a schmuck, crying, or would I be extremely happy and look like the cat that swallowed the canary? I was praying Tommy would show up. I must say that I still had my doubts.

I went around the corner, down the hall and headed towards the secluded locker area Tommy and I shared innocently since our freshman year. My heart was racing. I was full of adrenaline and now found myself walking at a faster pace. I went around the last row of lockers and towards mine. And there he was! He waved for me to hurry up and get over there. So with my hall pass in hand, I hustled over to him. He put his hands on my arms and looked directly in my eyes. I felt soooo warm and fuzzy! Oh man…I was sure I was melting into those buff biceps! I don't remember breathing! He spun me around and got really close with his body to mine. I was now up against the last row of lockers. We were hidden. I couldn't take my eyes off of him. He took his hands and placed them on the back of my neck, cupping my head and face, and then he pulled me up closer to his angelic face. He kissed me so gently and slowly. His lips were soft and I found myself just continuing to melt into his arms as we started kissing more heavily. Our bodies were now tight against one another as we hugged and grabbed each other in a heat of passion making out like I had only ever been able to dream about before, or seen in a movie love seen. His hands had caressed my behind…so I thought… what the hell, why not! And then I grabbed a hold of his! And what fine butt cheeks he had! Our lips and tongues kept connecting in heavy breaths. He had a subtle moan that was actually making the experience more enjoyable for me, because it told me he was into how I was interacting with him. I too, made some little noises to let him know I was thoroughly enjoying our secret event. And when he started to kiss my neck…I thought I was going to lose it! I found my erogenous zone that day! Man! It seemed that we couldn't get enough of each other during those moments that seemed to be frozen in time and I was certain I didn't want it to end! I felt his erection as we stayed pressed against one another. He swept his hand across my ruffles and on to my breast, caressing it gently then firming his grip as we became more and more excited. I ran my fingers through his hair, grabbing hold of it as he was kissing my neck. I would also nibble and kiss his earlobes. This was by far the best encounter I could ever have asked for! My dreams didn't compare to the heated rendezvous that was now a reality. I didn't want it to end! I knew class would be over soon and the halls would then be filled with students. I pulled away from Tommy reluctantly and still kissing him and said "We need to get out of here before we get caught!" He still had a hold on me but agreed. My head was spinning. My body was hot, his was hot and a little sweaty at this point and we knew we had to gather ourselves and get back to class. We adjusted our clothes and fixed our hair. We were both catching our breath as I picked up my hall pass that had fallen to the floor at some point…I'm glad I found it! And

"DON'T TELL MOMMY"

I was mesmerized! We looked at each other as we walked side by side down the corridor to the main halls that led to our classes. He went one way down the hall. I had to go in the other direction. He whispered as he looked back, "Are you glad you came?" I looked at him and said "Ah, yeah!" Like duh Tommy! If he had only known *just* how much! If he had only known how his attention and sweet disposition that day gave me more hope for myself than I could ever imagine. Maybe in time he will know? I lost all sense of anxiety and all my worries had faded as we embraced for maybe about a total of 5-7 minutes. My 5-7 in heaven didn't happen in a closet at a party... it happened right there in the hall locker area...how cool was that!? I did realize we could get caught and for a while...I didn't care. But I also knew we were secretly meeting. I didn't want Tommy's friends to find out and he may end up regretting our little encounter. I definitely didn't want that to happen! I was overwhelmed with emotion in a way I never was before. I had kissed some guys before, but nothing compared to what went through me when I was kissing Tommy. It was telling me that *this is what it's supposed to feel like*! A guy and a girl...getting hot with one another...consensually...nothing forced... and surely nothing planned in a perverted, wicked manner. It made me feel like I was finally a *real* girl! And I liked it! How could I not? And I owed it all to Tommy.

Best day ever!

I now loved...loved, loved, and loved *our little secret!* Tommy and I would meet a handful of times, by our lockers and basically tongue wrestle and get all hot and bothered! It felt like we couldn't get close enough to one another in the corner section of lockers where we would meet. If we were found out...it would have been scandalous! I'm pretty sure it may have possibly been embarrassing for him, and I would once again return to being the awkward introverted and dorky chick I thought people perceived me as. I didn't want everyone saying things like, "Eeww...why would Tommy want to be with her?! Gross! She's a dog! Look at her clothes! Is he desperate or what?" Or even worse..."She probably offered to give him a blow job!" Whatever the backlash would be, I knew it wouldn't be positive! I didn't trust what anyone may spit off their forked tongues.

All was wonderful in my world of sneaky smooching...and then some. And then the news came on the morning announcements. Some brainiac butt lick came up with the new concept of having hall monitors! Ugh! The school administration had put in place tables and a few chairs at each stairwell on each level of the school. The purpose you may ask? The purpose was to check any wandering students for hall passes and be sure they were not trying to skip out on classes. Personally, I thought it was an excuse to give seniors yet another reason to feel superior in our school. Well isn't that special!? Poo!!! I thought for sure Tommy wasn't going to take that big a risk and continue to give me my little love notes to meet him for what had become our "make out sessions". Was I wrong??? Actually I was very happy to be wrong about something for a change! He actually *still* wanted to take the chance and be with me...knowing there is now a great risk of getting caught because there was a freakin' senior hall monitor sitting at the opposite end of the rows of lockers where we would meet! He still wanted to meet! I was elated, and a little nervous, but I went along with it because I hated the thought of our escapades ending. We met and I found myself being really paranoid and uncomfortable as we attempted to let our inhibitions fly like we had in past encounters, but it was really hard to walk past the hall monitor, show them our passes, separately of course, and the open our lockers as if we needed to retrieve something from them...then go at it hiding where the monitor couldn't see us! That was possible but being quiet was the hard part! Tommy and I could disappear from sight but not go unheard. The first time there was a monitor, we were fine. Our meeting was swift and nerve racking. We couldn't, I couldn't, relax enough to let the paranoia go and feel free to enjoy him as I had a few times before. It was definitely not the same. Tommy would tend to stick his tongue in my ear and I would squeal! I couldn't take that! Ick! It was hot that he even wanted to…but I was ticklish and freaked out when he would do that! I found it difficult to enjoy our *get togethers*. I told him I didn't think our meeting like that was going to work anymore. I felt we were eventually going to get busted and I didn't want that possible shame put on him. I also didn't want to have to explain a phone call to my parents as to why I had been assigned after school detention or whatever punishment the school may implement on me for doing something like that. My stepdad would have been pissed and would take it out on me in *his own special way* when no one was around. I was still haunted by his presence and demands. If he knew I had real feelings for a guy at school and found out that I did anything physical with him, I just knew he would flip out and make me do possibly worse things with him than I already had. He would try to convince me that I liked it because I was doing *naughty (not naughty when it's with someone outside of your family!)* … *touchy feely* things with a normal guy at school.

I obviously hadn't dated openly to my parents. I would have them drop me somewhere thinking I was meeting a girlfriend from school. Once in a blue moon it was to meet up with a guy. This guy. The ultimate guy in my eyes. Tommy and I knew meeting at the lockers was not a good idea any longer. One day I got an unexpected note from Tommy. I thought he understood that we couldn't designate a time to meet at our lockers any more. That didn't stop me from thinking about him day and night! (How the hell *did I* ever do so well in school with him on my mind???) So I was surprised when I read the note and he had asked me to meet him at the Stroud Mall for a movie one night. What?! Was this a date??? Here I go again…getting all anxious…OMG–I am my mother!…getting all worked up over something that didn't even happen yet! I don't remember if it was a night during the week or on the weekend. I knew guys and girls did some heavy petting in back rows of movie theatres! My girlfriends had told me so. I told him I would have to see if I could get a ride and I would let him know the next day if I could meet him there or not. I asked my mom if she could drive me to the mall so I could go to the movies with Emma. I told her Emma was going shopping with her mom at the mall and then she and I would go to a movie and I could get picked up after. Normally Emma's mom was kind enough to cart my ass around. She knew my family didn't have money for anything and she would always be very hospitable and kind to me. I was afraid my mom would question why Emma's mom wasn't bringing me home. Thankfully, this time she didn't ask.

The mall was crowded as I entered and saw the long lines for tickets at the movie theatre. So I'm thinking it probably was a weekend night. I wore a baseball style T-shirt that had baby blue ¾ length sleeves and a white body. There was a decal of Smurfette on the front. Yeah…pretty hot! Yikes! I also chose to wear my pair of Levi baby blue corduroy pants that were a little snug. With that I wore some used blue Nike sneakers. The style was similar to those we used for cheerleading. Like I said, I didn't have much to work with. It was so lame! I wished I had nice things to wear…especially for events as important as this one was to me. Tommy knew I was poor, but he still secretly liked me for some reason, and I was thankful.

So I get in line to buy a ticket and I started looking around for Tommy. I didn't see him. I purchased my ticket, which I believe was only about $4.00 back then, and as I walked around the corner…I saw him! I had a lump in my throat…he was so freakin' handsome! So I went from the line to buy tickets, then to the line to wait to get into the movie theatre and find seats. These lines were long! Way too long! Tommy was closer the front of the wait-to-get-in line but still there were many ahead of him. I however was now near the back of that stupid long line. The attendant let down the velvety rope and let awaiting people file in. Tommy motioned and said to me that he would go find seats. I just nodded back in an affirmative manner. Crap…here I go again! I felt a rush come over me. It was an oppressive feeling that gave me a panic attack as if I didn't realize what was really going on. I swear it was like something took over me. Something called fear I guess. As I

"DON'T TELL MOMMY"

slowly walked in the darkened theatre and saw the back probably 6 or 7 rows were already filled, I didn't see Tommy. I found myself in a daze of sorts. What was wrong with me??? It was hard to breathe and I guess I was just so nervous to be out in public with Tommy at a movie? Would someone from school be there and see us? It was pretty dark in there and then I saw him up ahead near the center left section of the theatre. The aisle went straight down the center splitting the seating into only 2 sections. I could see him looking back, and I froze. My heart was up in my throat and I pretended I didn't see him in the massive mix of people in the theatre. Why? Why why why why???!!! What the fuck is wrong with me!? I spotted a seat a few rows down from him on the opposite, right side of the theatre. It was a single seat in the middle of a row. I couldn't tell you who was on either side. I saw Tommy motioning to me like "I'm over here!" I pretended I didn't see him! He had saved me a seat right next to him. Why the heck didn't I go?! What was wrong with me!!!??? I was screaming at myself on the inside! I was panic stricken and *I couldn't go and sit next to the guy I had adored for years...WHY? What's wrong with me?!?!* I proceeded to crawl across some people and took the single seat. I sat still for a moment looking straight ahead and down at myself. I then looked up and pretended to look behind me in this dark room FULL of people. I gazed around quickly pretending that I was scanning for Tommy. I looked past him and continued to follow my eyes down to the front of the theatre. I was acting like *I was the one who couldn't find him.* He was raising and waving his arms...of course I saw him! What an ass! Me...not him! I then scanned back and I had to acknowledge seeing him. He couldn't come to me, there wasn't any room. He motioned for me to come over as he pointed to the empty seat next to him that he saved for me. I once again froze. The movie previews had started. I just looked at him and shrugged my shoulders as if... Oopsie! It's too late to move, the movie has already started. He just looked at me like "what the fuck girl?!" And I sat back and slouched way down in my seat. Hiding. Hiding from embarrassment of my inexplicable behavior. My bizarre way of showing Tommy how much I liked him…ha! How freakin' stupid could I be??? Pretty damn stupid it seemed! Ya' know…I couldn't even tell you what movie it was! I was so worked up I have no clue what movie I saw. That's because I didn't really see it. I just sat there like a jack ass with my head down sobbing the whole time. I was praying no one would notice I was crying. I have no flippin' idea what movie I had agreed to meet Tommy at. I was mortified and most definitely in a state of shock myself at my own behavior! I couldn't wait for the movie to end. I didn't even look back at Tommy. I acted like it was taboo to get up once seated and move to another seat. I acted like I would be arrested for changing seats in a freakin' movie theatre and it wasn't an option. BUT WHY? The movie was finally over! Now I dreaded seeing Tommy and having to explain my asinine dick move of ditching him. I was soooo upset. I sat for a while until the crowd had filtered out somewhat. I was worried about Tommy confronting me and I wouldn't really have a good explanation for him. I didn't have one for myself! I reluctantly looked back and across the theatre. He was gone. He was gone from his seat, but was he waiting for me outside? I walked out slowly as I kind of mixed myself in with some other people I didn't even know. If I had a tail…it would have been tucked down in between my legs! I walked with my head down and my eyes barely could see where I was walking as well. I shuffled my way outside the theatre and found myself in the middle of the mall. I didn't hear Tommy call out to me. I looked around quickly and hauled ass out through the glass doors and plastered myself against the side of the concrete walls on the building, where I had apparently just lost my freaking mind! I saw my mom in our unmistakably shitty car and ran into the parking area and jumped in the car. She asked "Where's Emma?" I explained to her that Emma felt sick and called her mom to pick her up early and I wanted to stay and finish watching the movie. I was lying through my crowded teeth! My mom assumed that we were dropping off Emma at her house. I was beside myself with disappointment. My mother asked me how the movie was. I said "It was okay." She didn't push any other questions on me…thank God! I wouldn't have had any

"DON'T TELL MOMMY"

answers for her. I would have to bullshit my way through, and hope not to get caught lying later. What had I done? I instantly hated myself. I was soooo distraught. It took all I had to not burst out crying in front of my mother on the ride home. I just couldn't wait to get to bed and curl up in a ball. Then, I could cry. Fuck.

Worst night ever.

CHAPTER **19**

Dumb Blonde

I DID CRY myself to sleep that night. I am glad my sister was not around and so I had our bedroom all to myself. I moped around the all the next day. I still didn't understand why I was such a jerk. How could I blow the chance to be on a real date with Tommy, even if we had still kept whatever we had…a secret? How dumb of me!? I was dreading going back to school on Monday morning. I did not want to face him. I had already regretted what I had done and didn't know what I would say to Tommy after the stunt I so ridiculously pulled at the mall. How does someone explain themselves for that kind of bizarre behavior? There goes that anxiety and panic mode again! I remember faking illness so I didn't have to go to school Monday. I was so scared and now I also became worried if Tommy would finally tell his friends that I was being a slut by throwing myself at him or I don't know…all these crazy ideas of how he could bash me went through my mind. I could possibly be worse than before he and I started fooling around. My life at school could become an even more tragic addition to my already shitty life! I was sick to my stomach, but not from any virus…it was over my own stupidity.

Well I had to go back to school sooner or later and face my crush whether I liked it or not. I went to school on Tuesday. Believe me,

"DON'T TELL MOMMY"

I tried to get out of going for another day but my mother wasn't buying it! So I went. I had wished I was truly invisible now more than ever. I know how I freaked out with the movie situation was a result once again, from the damage Jared had caused. My long time exasperated soul was something I was barely able to hang on to. I didn't feel like I had a purpose to exist in life until I felt like I was alive. This happened when I fell for Tommy. This happened when I experienced the kindness of Tommy, even though he may have been embarrassed to share that he had liked me AT ALL. That wasn't his fault. I blame the peer pressures that obviously even some of the crème de la crème at our school was exposed to as well. Not just the misfits. Expectations were set to basically be with those like you. It was a clique made up of those of a higher economic stature. Or those who had nothing, like me. And you were kind of expected to *hang with your own*. Once in a while you would see a couple that looked "miss matched". Like a stoner getting it on with an honor student for example. And of course people would talk! I hated that about the Poconos. It was widespread place, but everyone knew everyone else's business. Well anyone that *mattered*. No one questioned mine. So if the school had gotten wind that Tommy was smooching around with me… oh yeah…people would have talked and I believe would have ruined what Tommy and I had even more. So I didn't blame him for wanting secrecy. Like I said, I was just thankful he looked my way. My life had been a nightmare of constant fear, torture, chaos, and hatred since I was six years old. I never wanted my life to go on as it remained horrifying for years. The torture and tears never disappeared. Tommy and my friends I cherished at school were the only things that kept me going. And now I knew part of that little glimmer of hope and happiness was about to disappear, I just knew it.

School that day had me even sicker to my stomach than the day before when I had stayed at home. I went to my locker. I was glad to not have seen Tommy at his. I went to homeroom and almost made it through the day until I saw him. It was after the last class and everyone was spilling out into the halls in the mad rush to get the hell out of there! Tommy was with Don and a real goof ball named Richard. He was basically the class or maybe even the school clown. I liked him though. He and I would make fun of each other at least. It wasn't one sided and was truly in fun. So Tommy spotted me. My heart sank. I stood there. I stood still and let everyone else pass by and go around me. It was time to face him. I looked at him and mouthed "I'm sorry" silently while I once again shrugged my shoulders. He looked at me, stopped for a fleeting moment, and waved his arms down in that "forget you" fashion. Like…"get out of here"…know what I mean? "Forget about it". All those things relate to that motion. I knew what he meant. I knew loud and clear. It wasn't good, that's for sure. It was clear he now thought I wasn't worth his time, his touch, his tenderness. I fucked things up. I knew it. Damn it! And Jared was the underlying reason I just watched the most happy and heartfelt thing in my life shoo me away and literally walk out of my life.

I felt later, not at the time, but years later while in therapy that I was so afraid of anyone finding out about what was happening to me at the hands of my stepfather that I couldn't let anyone get close to me. I guess I feared if Tommy and I did turn out to be anything but a secretive fling, he would discover my secret and maybe the entire school would find out as well. I never gave it the chance. I knew deep down that I was damaged goods. I truly believed when I walked through my front door to that wretched house, I was a low life. I felt like I was scum, I was dirty, tainted, used goods, and definitely not worthy of the attention of hot popular guys. I wasn't choosing my own destiny. I was snapping to my harsh reality of what my life was…shit.

I avoided Tommy like the plague. I was humiliated knowing he thought I was some kind of basket case, a fuckin' freak…who meets someone out on a date, then goes and sits without him. Who does

"DON'T TELL MOMMY"

that? An insecure scared little girl, that's who does something as off the wall as that. That's who. Ugh. Things were never the same for me at school after the day Tommy tossed me aside.

Worst day ever.

CHAPTER **20**

I Grew a Pair?

I HAD LOST my faith in ever having who I truly wanted. I had my dreams and loving thoughts of others ripped out of me by my step monster. While I still clung to my school work and some friends I was also still trapped inside Jared's demented world. I know I had mentioned all that I felt my sister was seemingly doing with our dad. I again, am fuzzy on full details but I can tell you this next incident is only partially in my memory, as it was as bizarre as it was unthinkable at the time.

I don't know how it got to this point, or if it was day or night. I know I did not hallucinate ANY of what happened to me. I felt every bit of it. I found myself standing in my parents' bedroom. Jared was sitting naked on the bed and my sister was standing next to me. We were side by side, without any clothes on as if we were being judged on our bodies. I guess you could call it a comparison of sorts, by a sick fuck who had now pitted sisters to be against one another…and be anything but sisters, truly sisters, *ever* again. We were teens and our bodies had developed in ways a girl transforms into a woman. My sister Maureen was at a more advanced stage of evolution in this department compared to me. Of course I was in tears and my sister regretfully, was not. Jared was barking out orders to us. He did this in a manner as if it were a game of Simon Says. So the point I specifically remember was when Jared called out to my sister and me to face each other. Then he said "Now look at each other." I was a mess. Once again, I was an emotional train wreck, reluctant to participate in ANYTHING to do with Jared or my sister. But there I was, facing her with not a tear in her eyes. I don't know what I ever did to make her hate me so much. There's a good chance I never will, and now I may really never want to know. No explanation can excuse or be forgiven to convince me that I was genuinely loved by my sister and certainly not by my stepfather.

So as I am looking at my sister and witnessing the hate for me in her eyes, Jared's next command was to "put your hands on your sister's ass." My sister put her hands around me and on my bare ass so easily and immediately, as if it was rehearsed or something??? I didn't realize exactly what he was asking us to do, but apparently Maureen did. I jumped because she was now touching my naked ass, and it startled the crap out of me! Jared yelled "Do it!!!" in a deep, mean, scary as shit voice. I jumped again and was trying to lean away from my big sister as I begged for him to let me go. "Please don't make me do this" I said repeatedly! I was saying it over and over! I must have said it *at least* 5 times…and fast, like I was chanting it. My sister then yelled at me to my surprise. "Stop being such a fuckin' big baby, just do it! It's no big deal!" Um… **excuse me…bitch**…no big deal??? Who the fuck was she now to be giving me orders to do nasty things *with her???* I could have shit right there on the floor! I looked over at Jared who had already retrieved his tub of Vaseline out from under his bed. He was rubbing it all over his fuckin' dick that he must have thought was the greatest thing since…well since Vaseline! He too yelled at me again to "do it, or I'll make you get on your knees!" Crap…I didn't want that either. I didn't want to do anything…anything like this… EVER!!! He said calmly, "I'm waiting", and my sister squeezed my ass. Her nails had sort of dug into my skin. I thought I was going to throw up. So I leaned over and slowly started to put my arms around hers. I was hysterical. I guess I wasn't going fast enough because she yanked me closer towards her with her hands on my butt so I could reach her bare ass better. So my hands were now on my big sister's naked butt. Great. Just fuckin' great. So there we were. (Christ, that was so disgusting.) As if it wasn't bad enough, Jared then said…uh…"Give your sister a kiss." What?!? Are you fuckin' kidding me? She didn't seem to mind that command either. WHY??? "What in the world have these two been up to and why do I have to be included?" Is what was going through my mind. I would love to say it was all a just a nightmare, and then I woke up. I can't. As true as the love I have for my very own children, it happened. I was beside myself with grief, with the feeling of nothing but disgust and I didn't want to do any of this! My sister looked at me and said "Just stop it already, it'll be quicker if you just shut up and do what he says." Like it was no biggie. Eh, just lean on over here and give your fuckin' naked sister a kiss. I shook my head no. Jared was jerking himself off and was getting really annoyed with me as if I was spoiling all his fun. What a fuckin' asshole! He was clenching his lips together but said…"Do it". Like a grunt. I looked back at Maureen. All I could see was her big lips. Her lips were actually bigger than mine. I thought they were ugly, maybe because they were on her. I just closed my eyes. And then I felt my sister's fuckin' mouth plant a kiss on mine. I started screaming with my mouth closed! She stood there and did that for a few seconds. I didn't move. It was truly a grotesque moment that you wish would disappear from your mind, but you know it never will. I couldn't take it any longer! I pulled away from her and started to scream…"I fucking hate both of you!" I pushed Maureen out of the way and high tailed it out of the bedroom! I didn't know what may happen to me next. I didn't care. My give a damn was busted and I had finally busted out not caring if they would kill me then and there. I was sooo tired of being scared and tormented. The abuse occurred so often that I couldn't function at home in fear of being attacked at any time. Things at home were too unpredictable and

"DON'T TELL MOMMY"

I was feeling like I was losing my mind. I knew it was time. It was time to fight back harder than ever before. It was time for me to get smarter in how to avoid getting into these sadistic situations that had eaten me alive. I felt like there wasn't much left of me.

CHAPTER **21**

Sweet Dreams Are Made of *This*...Asshole!

I HAD DREAMED of many ways that I could put fear into the sick individual who had been sexually assaulting me since I was a little girl. Martin Luther King wasn't the only one who had a dream folks! I had several of my own and I am about to "Release the Kraken", so to speak and share *my disturbed side,* which I guess anyone may have, having experienced all that I did too.

*Please keep in mind that this comes from a person who went through *extreme* hell. I was a child, helpless and destroyed by a fucking monster! Don't judge my dreams. I am not a violent person by far! Hell, I even apologize to a spider or a fly before I have to kill it! (I don't do bugs...sorry! ;-x) So just remember...these are only dreams!

Eat shit and die? Na...way too humane. I would have visions sometimes, wonderful visions of terrible things happening to my former stepfather. In fact, not that long ago I was talking to my mom on the phone, as I do almost on a daily basis, and I told her I had a dream the night before. I had a dream that involved Jared dying some horrific death while he was chasing me down. She replied, "So you had a nightmare?" I had to say it again and explain this one more time to her that "Mom, *anytime* I see shit bad happening to Jared in my sleep, it's a good thing! It is a *DREAM,* NOT a nightmare!" I didn't mind having those dreams. I actually found comfort in imagining that it could possibly be true. Like I said, I can dream can't I?

I had sweet thoughts of his stupid truck, the one he would take me for our little rides in, I dreamed he would veer off the side of Fountain Road, down an embankment, and ram into a tree, having the branch come through the windshield and go straight through his head.

I had a recurring dream that Jared would be chasing me through the cemetery up the road from our house at night. I would hide behind a tall tomb stone. As he crept close to me I pushed him hard and he landed on the grave next to him...getting impaled by a crucifix right through the middle of his body where his heart was *supposed* to be.

I would have bits and pieces of dreams of me busting in on Jared as he was jerking off in the bath tub and slicing his penis and scrotums off and stuffing them in his mouth and in his own ass. No search party for the penis in the woods needed! ☺

I had some delightful thoughts of shooting him with a 22. (That was the rifle I could shoot growing up.)...Directly in his crotch, and then leaving him in the woods to bait the bears. They would tear him to shreds and devour him while he was still alive! Awesome!

Another goodie, and one of my favorites by far because it was like a mini movie...this one is in depth and the most recurring one of all of them. There are many more, too many. I feel upon telling you will now fully understand how *I wanted to now make him feel.* I have some dreams that are so vivid that I wake up thinking, "Wow, did that really happen? It felt like it!" I wanted so desperately to turn the tables on him. I wanted him to feel fear and pain, even if it was only in my dreams.

I was being chased by Jared through our scary old house. I was fully clothed in my cheerleading uniform, saddle shoes and all! (Yes, we still had them in the 80s!) And Jared was nude, shocking, I know… ugh. He chased me as I ran from my parents' bedroom trying to escape another event of insane abuse. I ran down the hall and around the banister and went down the steep stairs. I flew around the corner and went into the pantry. There I would find one of Jared's favorite fishing knives used for gutting. I grabbed it from the deep white porcelain sink and I held it tight. I heard his pounding footsteps coming down the stairs. I knew he wasn't that far away. He stopped at the bottom of the staircase. He had 2 choices. He could go left and into the living room or he could go to the right, which would take him to the kitchen, then through to the pantry…and to me. I was crouched down by a freestanding cabinet just inside the open doorway. The light from the moon lit my sight just enough to be able to see in front of me. Other than that, it was completely dark. The old wide wood floor boards were now creaking under the worn vinyl floor covering in the kitchen. He was coming for me. He walked slowly like a stealth panther, and then I saw his silhouette coming through the pantry doorway.

As he stepped into the moon light, through the bare side window, I let him have it! I rammed that knife with the curved side down into the back of his leg, just above the back of his knee. I held on to that knife as he wailed in pain. He fell face down on the pantry floor just missing hitting his face on the washing machine. I put both my hands on the grip of the knife and pulled down as hard as my body could! Jared's scream could have wakened the dead! I was now the one who was fuckin' pissed and full of rage! I ripped that fuckin' knife down and into the back of his knee. My feet were braced against the side of his stubby, hairy body. I loudly shouted at him "How does that feel, you son of a bitch!?!" He continued to scream and was trying to grab the knife but he couldn't twist and reach it. Aaaahhh, poor baby! Fucker! He began to slap at me as I held on to that knife. I said, "What's wrong daddy, can't you get up???" I now had taken on the role of some demonic psycho myself…and I was loving it! I would say, "Oh no, no, no daddy...you shouldn't try to take my knife away from your little girl." He was moaning and flailing about on the floor. Blood was all over the floor. He would scream "Give me that, you little bitch!" Oh, did he just say what I think he did? "Well daddy, you shouldn't try to take things from me!" I yanked the knife out of his leg and slammed in into his left hand! Wheeeew! I was so empowered in this dream! I was in control now! I slammed that knife into his hand so hard that it went right through his hand and it stuck into the pantry floor! (Awesome, I know!) Man, now *he* was screaming like a little girl! I wanted him to suffer something awful. Even if for one night. One night compared to more than a decade that I had endured his fuckin' nasty ass abuse...oh...he was in for it! (Remember, this is one of my fantasies...it wasn't real.L) So now I had him down, but he was still able to move. I couldn't have that! So next I retrieved *my little buddy*, the fishing knife, and I got up and stepped down on his arm with my foot and bent over and pulled it from the floor and out of his hand...slowly. It must have been serrated on the blade somewhere because I could gear his flesh rip as I slowly sliced back on his hand as I pulled it out. The big bad boogey man was laying face down on the floor, bleeding, making the damn floor slippery...and I wasn't done with him yet! I hopped over his sorry ass and opened the cellar door. I pulled the string that was attached to a single uncovered light bulb, and then tossed the knife down the worn wooden steps. These were the steps that led to what was next to now become *Katelyn's torture chamber*. Oh...it gets even better!

I looked back over at Jared. He was only about 2 feet away. He was attempting to use his right hand and leg to get up. "I wouldn't try that if I was you Daddy!" I went over to him and jumped down on his arm. I braced myself by holding on top of the washing machine. I jumped up and down as hard as I could in my little red pleated cheerleading skirt and hard soled saddle shoes. I was basically using his right arm as a mini tramp and was leaning on the washer for balance.

Reminds me of how I practiced my cheer jumps on the front porch.

SWEET DREAMS ARE MADE OF THIS...ASSHOLE!

Hhhhhhmmmm. So I was having a blast pouncing up and down, twisting from side to side, almost as if it was a little dance. A happy dance for this rah-rah! He was making too much noise and I needed him to shut the fuck up! I was hoping to break his fuckin' arm in many places.

I was in the pantry. I looked over at the old high back white porcelain sink and see a Brillo pad that's been used probably for dirty pots and pans. I grabbed that, it was nice and yucky! I hopped back over to fuck face that was still on the floor. I pulled his head up by his hair, he yelled naturally, so he made it easy for me to stuff the Brillo pad way down in his foul mouth! I grabbed one of his tube socks that was in a pile of dirty laundry on top of the brown colored washer, and fuckin' tied that sock around his head, gagging him even more as it kept that now...multi-purposed Brillo pad trapped inside his mouth. Who knew? I was psyched now! "Eh-eh-eh-eh"...that's all he could mutter from his newly stuffed trap of a mouth. I took a heavy pan that was in the drying rack on the sink and wacked the shit out of him in the back of his head! Yeah...just like in the movies! I kicked at him and pushed him over on his back. I knocked him out! Woo hoo! I grabbed the other sock and tied his arms and started tugging at him, pulling him by his bound wrists, to get him closer to the cellar stairway. I was giggling and thoroughly enjoying myself! (Evil, I know and that was new for me!) I was now ready for the next phase.

I was like Wonder Woman possessing great strength, and I mirrored Norman Bates with my mind. I dragged Jared's wounded, lifeless stub of a body over to the top of the cellar stairs. He was still knocked out and his eyes were closed. Good thing because he didn't want see what was coming! I folded him over, and just *HEAVED* and pushed his ass down the cellar stairs! He rolled and bounced a little. If he would have been conscious, his dick and ball sack would have been probably what hurt most! Haha!...It flipped about and it all got squashed as he hit the stairs as he went down. I trotted down the stairs as he landed on the concrete floor in our creepy basement. I dragged him around the corner where Jared and others would skin and process freshly hunted deer. There was a heavy support beam that ran from the end of the stairs all the way over to the wall. On that support beam was a pulley system to hoist up the largest of game at Jared's mercy. I pulled another string that turned on another single bulb that hung loosely from the ceiling. Usually he shot big ass bucks, does, and occasionally some smaller animals as well. He did it out of season as well. It was our main source of meat throughout the year.

So, the pulley was there. I wrapped the rope around his already bound wrists and intertwined the rope so he surely could not get free. He was unconscious anyway. I, the Wonder Woman that I had become, picked up the other end of the rope and went to the middle of the cellar floor where there was a drain in the floor to hose blood and unwanted carnage from the gutted animals. I hoisted him up until he was hanging unable to touch the cold cellar floor. I took another piece of rope that was hanging around and used it to tie his ankles together, making a figure 8 and wrapping tightly around and around so he would never break free. Jared was now coming out of his state of unconsciousness. There he was, hanging by his double bound wrists above his head. His head hung down. It wasn't bleeding...*yet*. I wacked him hard and he was dazed but not confused. He was well aware of who I was. He started trying to scream. I wasn't about to free his tongue to allow him to verbally lash out at me...*yet*. I would say, "Welcome back daddy! You took a little nap there." I could tell he was hurting, and I was smiling. I walked over to the other side of the stairs where I then found the fishing knife I tossed down the steps earlier. I b-bopped around playfully after being reunited with *my little buddy*. I appeared in front of Jared as he seemed to be very agitated. I asked "What's wrong daddy? Is something bothering you?" I was speaking to him as if he was a little insignificant boy. He could only mutter and grunt. Oh...my bad! His mouth was stuffed with Brillo and he was gagged with a dirty tube sock, poor baby! I assured him to hold on, and I told him I'll take the sock off. I pulled over a red metal step stool. I went behind him with my new buddy, *his* former fishing knife that I claimed as my own now. I wiped the blood off of it on to the tube sock hanging down in the back. I then slid the knife up in between his swollen head and the sock then roughly sawed away at the tube sock. I tied myself a good tight gag back there, and that was for sure! He was trying to yell because it hurt. (Oh, how my heart pumps nothing but piss for you, Jared…you piece of shit!) So I got the sock off and he was coughing, gagging, trying to get the Brillo out of his mouth. He was wiggling around, *as if* he could free himself from me. I slapped his ass and said "Now stop moving like that or I'll have to spank you harder daddy." He was choking on the steel wool pad, so I pulled my cute red step stool around to the front of him, being careful to not get too close to him where he *could* possibly try something, but doubted that that fortunate opportunity would never arise…it was MY dream!) I stepped up with my little buddy in hand, and I aggressively grabbed his face with my left hand. I squished his mouth as hard as I could and said "Open wide!" With my knife in my right hand and my left holding his face still, his mouth was open. I stuck the curved tip of the knife in his mouth saying "You better open wide or this knife won't fit and if I cut you, it will be your own fault!" (Eeeewww, slicing someone's lips open vertically…that's something I *should* have dreamed of doing, but I didn't.) So he opened up some, allowing the tip of the knife to catch the disgusting Brillo pad that was lodged in the back of his mouth. I slowly pulled it out and flung it off the knife and it went flying across the cellar. I stepped down. He was coughing and gagging. He spit at me. Oooohh…that made Miss Katelyn very, very, mad! "Poor daddy, did that nasty Brillo pad taste yucky?" Well hell, I knew how to take care of that. I nudged my stool back over in front of him yet again. I stepped up so we were eye to eye. I grabbed his face one more time. I squeezed harder than before. I looked towards his mouth and said "I think I may have missed a piece." Good ole dad started to shake his head no. I suggested that I was pretty sure I still see something in there! I yelled "Open your fuckin' mouth!" It opened. I quickly grabbed his tongue and pulled it out as far as I could and stuck my little buddy right up through the center. Gotcha'! I enjoyed seeing that grown man cry. Scream...oh my goodness! I guess it hurt a little more than if he had bitten his tongue on accident while jerking off. I twirled that sucker and had half of his fucking tongue hit the floor! (It seems that karma can be sweet in dreams too.) I looked around and said "Oh man, mom is gonna' be pissed if I make a mess down here! And with that being said I stepped down to the floor and picked up his tongue. I looked behind me and there it was. Jared's handy dandy meat grinder just waiting for a little action on the stainless table. This machine was huge and it always scared me! Not in this dream! Jared and others would skin the animals, butcher them into sections, and then grind the meats to make sausages or burger... blablabla. Well I was ready to make my own ground meat! I had all the ingredients I needed already in the cellar ;-). I had seen it done before, so I knew it would be a little noisy, but I was confident that I could handle the task at hand, my hand this time. Jared was bleeding profusely from his mouth. Aawww, he couldn't *say* how badly it hurt! (Haha) I looked at him and said with excitement, "We won't be making any venison anymore!" (I hated it. I always had to eat it. All parts of it, even pickled deer heart...but that was actually good! I didn't know any better! I was a kid and got my ass beat if I didn't do as I was told!)

Anyway, pops was hanging out, literally, genitals and all, and getting a little more nervous it seemed, if that was even possible. (One can only hope.) I told him he needed to "settle down or this was going to be very difficult and I wouldn't want to slip and cut something that I probably shouldn't." He wasn't behaving himself! Ugh, now what to do. Ah ha! I looked over and like a song going off in my head, it sang to me. The hook! Of course, the giant meat hooks were hanging from the support beam, just waiting to get a hold of something too! (Ya' like that?!) So little Miss Suzy cheerleader possesses those Wonder Woman powers and with her little stool and her mighty strength, pulls one of the giant meat hooks over so it is directly adjacent to Mr.

SWEET DREAMS ARE MADE OF THIS...ASSHOLE!

Squirmy pants...oh right, no pants, anyway he would have shit them, if he had some on! Man his eyes grew to the size of golf balls! Never saw someone's eyes get so big! They were downright creepy! I told him to close his eyes, relax! He insisted on freakin' out and made lots of noise. Well I had about enough of this joker. I walked over to the wall where all the fishing rods and tackle boxes were on the dusty wooden shelves. I had to clear a few spider webs out of the way to get to anything. I fuckin' hated spiders! But it was like...no biggie! I got this! (No longer any sense of fear there in my dream!) And I searched through one of his *prized* boxes that none of us kids was ever allowed to touch. Heaven forbid we touch some of his junk! So I found some nice sized fishing hooks. I was like, "Oh cool! I got two that match!" (IDK...it's a dream.) So I took the pretty hooks and cut some line and tied one on each end. Then I took the hooks on the line and tied it to one of the rods that was on the shelf. It was red. (Maybe because red was my favorite color?) I walked over to *Danglin' Daddy* and saw he was still being a Mr. Squirmy with his eyes all buggin' out of his head. So with my trusty step stool, and my new contraption I made, like an evil MacGyver, I proudly displayed the hooks for Jared to see. He had no idea what I was about to do or did he see it coming???

Well it was the last thing he ever saw because I hopped right up there and hooked those fuckin' ugly ass eye balls of his right through his eyelids! Damn! I was fast and accurate! Boom, boom...done! I can't even bait a hook with a worm on a line these days! Ick...

I jumped off my pretty red stool and reeled that fucker's eyeballs in! I reeled them in as if they were a giant bass that weighed 200 pounds! I pulled, and cranked that reel...until finally...pop. Then pop again. There they were! Two ugly hazelish colored eyes and the eyelids to boot...an added bonus! Off to the grinder they will go. They got stuffed in on top of his tongue. This was going to be quite the gourmet blend isn't it? I saw he was not happy, not at all. But he was still alive and kicking! This man just could NOT be still. Shame on him. He *still* needs to be punished. Will he ever learn?

"DON'T TELL MOMMY"

I get up on my step stool. I pulled the meat hook over to him as close as I could get it to the pulley. And then with my Wonder Woman power, I hoist him up and ram his back on to the meat hook. He hung a little crooked, mind you, but I don't think he noticed. ♩ To think of all the poor deer who hung there before him. Tisk tisk. That man made such a squeal! You would have thought I hung a greased pig or something??? That reminds me of what happens next, you see. (A little fun with words.) I'm entitled!

It was time to finish my magical mix of customized meat, gourmet style; I called it "filet of Jared". So I simply grabbed his ball sack and with a fierce swoop of the fishing knife, I sliced his nuts and tossed them right into the grinder! Then without hesitation I grabbed that greased pig's only remaining weapon, his fuckin' shriveled dick…and "off with his head!" Okay, it wasn't quite a Marie Antoinette moment and I took the whole thing, but that did sound funny! And it *wasn't* so easy. Yep, that man was into the Vaseline again! I guess I had hooked a greased pig after all! My gourmet blend was complete. And so was my dream. It never went any further. It sounds longer than it happens in my sleep, I think???

So that's all she wrote my friends, as far as the most prominent of dreams I have had over many years. That is my fondest form or torture I think I have, *and remember*, it is only in my dreams. I had saved the best for last. Bon appetite! (Sorry.☺)

I know how all things are relative in my dreams when I remember certain things he had done to me. Some things leave a big impact, while others do not. My brain will never be able to fully comprehend and decipher what was in his demented, sick mind. Never.

CHAPTER **22**

My First? ☺

I AM PROUD to announce to all you fine readers, that I did find love within that mixed up; fucked up world I lived in. His name was Brock Savares. He was smart. He was very cute. He looked a lot like John Taylor from Duran Duran, who I adored in the eighties! He was thin, but not as thin as I was. (Remember, ass has to be bigger than mine!) He was a good athlete. He was a freakin' GREAT guy! We were seniors, and I don't even know how it happened, but we fell in love. I actually now had the balls to bring a guy over to my shit hole of a house, and Brock didn't care! He was amazing and never judged me. How is this possible??? I don't know! All I knew was that I think my stepfather saw that Brock wasn't *going to go away*. Jared actually started backing off from the ugliness of the sexual encounters he so frequently forced on me. Was I dreaming??? I was always leery of Brock discovering that ugly part of my life and be disgusted. I was so scared but I didn't let that stop me this time, not like I did with Tommy. Brock was on the quiet side as well. Shy around most people and was goofy enough to make me laugh in our time together. That time together grew more and more. We were one of those couples smooching out in the halls of PMHS…and Brock didn't feel ashamed to be seen with me! Amazing, I know!

Brock gave me the confidence I needed just in time to end high school on a high note! We spent every moment we could together. His dad did photography I believe, and he had a beautiful new wife. I think Brock's mom had died. He has a gorgeous sister who was very popular. (In fact...my ex husband even dated her!) There was a lot of sneaking in and out of windows back then! We had fun. The time came where Brock and I took our physical relationship to the highest level. Sex. I will tell you this...I was freakin' scared out of my mind for a couple of reasons. One was that I thought he may discover I wasn't a virgin, and I had been claiming I was. In my mind I was. But would he be able to tell? Another reason was that okay...I'm just going to say it. Brock may have been a skinny guy...but he had a fuckin' huge penis! Yep, he did! Ouch is all I could think of! It was twice the size of what Jared's was...and Jared's would hurt with trying to force it inside me. So how much pain would I be in with this sizable appendage of Brock's??? We actually tried several times, and it was just too painful...and there were definitely terrorizing memories flashing back. Awful memories. This wasn't going to be easy. Jared had left me alone for quite some time now...but the reminder of his presence was always there. I practically lived at Brock's house our senior year. I'm so glad his family liked me! And Brock was so thoughtful. He would buy me things. Things that meant something. He was a sweetheart. My official *high school sweetheart*!

So months probably had gone by and we were still trying and trying to achieve actual full blown intercourse. (No pun intended.) One night we were actually at my house and making out on the couch with blankets above and below us. The petting became quite heavy. Everyone was upstairs and in bed. My step monster included. Brock NEVER pressured me, and was more than patient! He was a freakin' saint! I think I was the one who got fed up with my own wining and bitching about how *it* hurt. I just said fuck it! (Again, no pun intended!) I said..."Let's just do this and get it over with!" It was my come to Jesus moment! How was this going to turn out???

He of course kept asking if I was sure. I said yes. I was wearing his football jersey, a little ironic I suppose, and I just bore down and said in a loud whisper "Do it!" And with that being said he trusted that big fleshy torpedo inside me! We both actually heard a "pop"! HOLY SHIT! I WAS IN SUCH FUKIN" PAIN! It took all I had to not scream bloody murder as he stayed as still as he could...because he knew it fuckin' hurt! Tears just poured down my face. It was an uncontrollable, involuntary reaction at that point. I couldn't help myself. He stayed there for a moment, and I said in a shaky voice, "Did you hear that?" He said "Yeah, are you ok?" with concern. I replied "I don't know", and "I think you should get off of me...GO SLOW!" I couldn't move. My coochie was on fire and throbbing...and NOT in a good way! Brock retrieved and we both were sort of in shock I think. There was a decent amount of blood, unlike before. I was in pain but relieved that I was truly a virgin??? Is that possible? Can a girl have lost their virginity at a young age and her hymen actually grows back? Or by some miracle did Jared never enter me while I had any blackouts??? I didn't know what was up! This craziness was running through my mind! Poor Brock. He had no clue of what that moment truly meant for me! Now he might. (Sorry for talking about your penis Brock, but I'm sure your wife is very happy!) This was pivotal to my story. I needed to experience an act so intimate with someone. An act that actually meant something to them as well. Know what I mean? I needed to be in love, love him, and I did. I loved Brock and I was glad to say I lost my virginity to him. That's my story and I'm sticking to it! I was a virgin until 1984, because I won't allow Jared to possibly take that away from me...even if it's only in my mind. He can't touch that now.

Needless to say, I WAS a virgin until Brock. I was seventeen and almost made it out of my senior year staying one. I was a rare breed at school. Pretty much all the other girls I knew had already lost their virginities...some long before. I was glad I waited. I was glad it was Brock. I was even gladder the next time, and the many times after that...that it didn't hurt nearly as bad as the first time! We both learned to enjoy sex and experimented with one another. It was fun because we cared about each other. That saved me. I had moved out with some friends I met the summer after graduation. After that I had gone away to college. Brock and I didn't make it, long story…maybe you can find out in my next book?

CHAPTER **23**

The Apple Doesn't Fall Far From the Tree, Does It?

I DON'T KNOW much about pedophilia as far as if it is a hereditary thing, or if it's a high percentage that if someone was a victim of a pedophile themselves as a child that they are more likely to put that pain on another living soul. That's for the experts to disclose. I do know, unfortunately, that Jared was not the only one in his family with this *illness*. I'll just keep calling it that for now, but by far is always going to be labeled a heinous crime.

I was probably twelve or maybe a little older and I went up to the bungalow on the property where my step grandparents lived. It was only an acre away. There was a worn path in the grass that led from our metal gate out in the backyard, passing the outhouse, and leading to my Grammy and Grand pop's front porch. It was small and smelly. They were not very clean people. There was always some kind of junk lying around outside. The inside was even worse. It had an odor that I can only explain as damp, musty, unclean, unsanitary, and offensive. I never like being around either one of them, my so called *Grandparents*. They too, smelled offensive and distinctive, that of body odor and bad breath. It was as if they hadn't bathed even maybe once a week. It was seriously foul.

◄ "DON'T TELL MOMMY"

I don't know why I needed to go up there that one afternoon. I have burned in my brain an image that can never be erased. I remember stepping up onto the covered screen porch, the screens were severely torn, dirty crap was everywhere, and the flies were everywhere. The worn out wooden boards creaked as I slowly approached the front door. There was a screen door that had to be opened first. I opened it slowly and lightly tapped on the distressed painted entry door. I didn't hear anyone answer my light knocking, but I knew someone was home. The old truck was parked by the big tree in the shade just across the way. So I took it upon myself to open the closed, but not locked, front door slowly and quietly. If Grammy or Grand pop was napping, I didn't want to wake them. I opened the door, very quietly, and just poked my head around it to see into the kitchen. What I saw will disgust me for the rest of my life! I saw her! I saw Maureen on her knees in front of our "Grand pop" sucking his dick. They were right there, plain as day…in the kitchen near the doorway to the main bedroom where he and Grammy slept. Grand pop was wearing his blue work uniform…and his pants *weren't* down, but it was obvious his zipper was open and my fuckin' sister was going to town on what *should have been kept in his pants*! Was she enjoying doing the dirty deed??? I didn't hear her crying or complaining. That was highly disturbing!

How do you process that one?! Christ, now my Grandfather was doing this sick shit too!!!??? It wasn't like he was a strapping young fellow. It wasn't like he was even a clean, pleasant looking or smelling being! He was nasty! He smoked cigars and pipes…worked as a mechanic for a dealership in Stroudsburg, Pennsylvania for years…he was always smelling of smoke,grease, and body odor! What the hell!? He saw my face. He fuckin' looked at me, smiled, grabbed the back of Maureen's head and made her go faster. (I am seriously gagging and ready to throw up as I am writing this!) She was so *preoccupied* that she did not know that I was even there. But good ole Grand pop did! And he acted as though he was boasting at what he had in front of him. I about choked on my own heart that went up into to my throat, I thought I was going to vomit on the spot! I looked down and slowly backed out of the door I had opened. I closed it and the screen door oh so quietly. I tip toed off the porch...and ran like my ass was on fire to my own house that I hated so much!

Well now that little dirty ole secret was out. Just to me? I don't know. I never mentioned that to Maureen. Had Jared and his father discussed the *added lifestyle* they seemed to now have shared??? Was I going to have to freak out about being around Grand pop now too? Damn straight I would! Jared's bullshit abuse was bad enough! To have my Grand pop do disgusting sexual things to me too was too much to bear. I *NEVER* went into their dumpy bungalow alone again! I know I made certain. Was I worried that Maureen and Grand pop would try to include me in their filthy escapades? You betcha'! I avoided that place and thankfully, someone must have been watching over me... once again...but I can't remember a time when Grand pop touched me inappropriately. I know I never gave him the chance after that day. But did he take his secret to his grave??

CHAPTER **24**

It's All in the Family

SO HOW LONG had horny old Grand pop been getting some action from my sister? Was Grammy not giving him any and he sought sex out elsewhere? Did Jared tell him Maureen would *do things for him* if he gave her money? I don't know. Only Maureen can answer that as Grand pop died years ago. Maureen has always refused to discuss, let alone acknowledge any of this sick fuckin' behavior that went on with her. She's mastered the art of lying and denying. She continues to believe her own lies. She's never gotten help for herself, and no one can make her. Is this her own doing, or was it all forced, programmed. Was she programmed to be a sex addict herself? Like a prostitute. Gross. Let's move on.

I had already moved out of my house of horror at the time that I was informed that my Grandfather had been *making moves* on my cousin, Miranda way back when she was just a little girl! My Uncle Ben and Aunt Connie supposedly confronted Grand pop about it, I was told, and then they ended up moving off the property out of their trailer and built a house. Miranda was younger than I was. I knew my aunt and uncle didn't come around much. My mom just thought they felt they were *too good* for the rest of us because they had more money. We never knew *their little secret*. My stepdad had worked for my uncle for a long time. Why did they decide to keep this information of incest a secret from the rest of the family??? Could some horrible things have been prevented if the *talking about it* had begun many, many years ago starting with outing Grand pop??? My mom wasn't told about the shit with her father-in-law until I told her about Jared, and I was eighteen! WTF?

Why didn't Grand pop come after me? Or did he...and I just don't remember? Did Jared tell Grand pop that I was far from willing and I wouldn't be an easy target? Did Jared tell him I would be a handful and maybe he wouldn't succeed? Did Jared assure *his daddy* that my sister didn't mind??? After the last incident I had with Jared that involved Maureen, things had slowed down. Things meaning the amount of times Jared would make/take serious advances towards me. Were Jared and Maureen finally scared that I would *out them*? Did they possibly think I thought they were bluffing or I simply didn't give a shit anymore if they did follow through on any death threats??? I say they because once my sister agreed to be a part of the sadistic acts, she became just as bad as Jared. Did she ever try to protect her little sister??? I don't know. I don't think so. She never mentioned a word to me about shit. No warnings, no sisterly advice. Fucked up, that's all I can say. We never talked about it. Would the shit with Jared and Maureen stop forever???

I was never told details about what happened with Miranda. Like I had said soooo many times before. That type of shit wasn't up for discussion back then. I am thankful Miranda had the strength to speak out against her own flesh and blood Grandfather. I am even happier that my step aunt and uncle believed her! But did they ever think he may move on to the next victim? Were there threats thrown at her putting her family in physical danger? I don't know that either. I am just glad she was able to rid herself of the family fungus. I hope she wasn't permanently damaged and was able to lead a somewhat normal life. She had a brother we called Little Ben. I hope nothing happened to him. Same as my brothers. Did anything sinful ever happen to them???

CHAPTER **25**

Oh Boy?!?

I WILL TELL you straight up that I do not know for sure if my brother Todd or my half brother Jr. was ever molested by Jared or Grand pop. I *do* remember my mom talking about how my brother Todd would have extremely painful bowel movements. So painful that he would scream in excruciating pain while going to the bathroom. He was about eight years old I believe. My mother wanted to take him to the doctor because she knew that wasn't *normal*. I think Todd freaked and begged for her to NOT take him to see a doctor. It could have been for several reasons. It could have been from hemorrhoids. My mom checked him out herself for that and didn't see any. I guess she knew what to look for…what lengths moms will go to! But she said he was all red and sore at his anal area…sorry Todd…and she just chalked it up to him maybe being constipated and he had been taking some hard poops. Did she ask Todd if someone had been violating him back there? No. That wasn't something really thought of or talked about. She didn't suspect anything like that until after she learned of my ordeal when I was in college. I have asked Todd several times to this day and he swears that Jared never did anything sexual to him, but my mom and I still have our doubts. My bro is six feet two and has been incarcerated in one way or another since he was about twelve.

I distinctly remember Daddy Dearest beating the shit out of Todd quite often. He literally just picked at him, provoking him to get angry then took that as a reason to justify beating the shit out him. Jared was *AWFUL* to my brother Todd! I would try and get in the middle sometimes to make Jared stop pounding on him or kicking him when he would knock him down on the ground. So needless to say Todd ran off a lot. It was brave of him because he was so young. He is 2 years younger than I am. I don't blame him! I wished I could have run away! I packed a bag a time or two. Chicken shit, yes I was. I knew Jared would find me somehow.

Todd ran, but to the wrong people. He ended up hanging out with another family known to be rednecks as well…we'll call them The Schreiber's. They had a few kids…okay maybe four as well, and were known to be a bit bad ass. The girls had foul ass mouths, like my sister, and the parents had the reputation of just having no control over their kids. Maybe they chose not to. But Todd would always seem to find trouble with some of those boys and they would get caught! They would do stupid shit. They would drink at a young age and smoke weed too I think. Then they would go steal four wheelers and go joy riding, things like that. I think they would put them back, but the owner didn't appreciate what they were doing and pressed charges. That's how I remember it starting. Todd's life as a *career criminal*.

I blame it on our dad. #1…our real, biological dad. If he had been a real man and been around for his kids, we may not have lived a life of hell on earth. We will never know. He can fuck off too, piece of shit. #2…our stepdad. He who swept in and *owned* our lives as we knew them to be, horrifying and insane. Either way, my brother Todd turned to a life of drugs and stupid crimes that led to worse things. He is actually due to get out of prison the end of next month. I'll talk more about his troubles in my next book…there has to be a sequel! People need to know how to handle and possibly get through this fucked up shit without hanging themselves, so there will be another book, if y'all will have me!

CHAPTER **26**

But Wait...There's More

MORE EVIL THAT is. As I stated earlier, the sessions with Satan and his mistress Maureen had seemed to dwindle. I was a senior in high school now. I was seventeen. Thank God! I am NOT complaining! Did Jared still try stupid shit? Yes, of course, like any sick sex addict pedophile would be expected to. He would, I feel, purposely, keep our already drafty house seriously cold. My mom would keep these ugly afghans around that our Grammy would make. I think she kept them only because Grammy would get pissed if she didn't see them on display when she would come over.

Well Jared had become very daring and tried to touch me when I had an afghan on while napping on the couch...with other people around sometimes! I would kick the shit out of him as I sometimes caught him sticking his hand or his head under my cover. What an idiot! It was obvious while I was growing up that *he wasn't right*. He was a dumb shit and sick bastard. He had no remorse for destroying the lives of others, human and otherwise. That cruel asshole would take an unwanted litter of kittens and tie them one by one to a tree, and shoot them. Shoot them as if he was sporting his guns in target practice! Our animals weren't *fixed* as they say. We could barely afford to have one, let alone take proper care of any pets! He had also been known to put puppies or kittens in a bag full of rocks. Tie the bag tight, and throw them in the creek so they would drown horribly! He was proud of himself. Proud of being fucked up I guess.

But wait...there's more! My mother explained the main reason why she was *for* the divorce...finally! She had finally realized Jared had been fooling around with some skank named Glenda at work. Where he worked at then, I don't know. I was a pleasant 4 hour drive away at school when I found this shit out! So she confronted him and he didn't deny it! Oh...what you fuckin' pussy...grow a pair now and hurt my mom in this manner!? *I was furious!* This woman had a freakin' mustache and everything. She was masculine in her face, ugly as sin. My mother busted her ass for him...for her kids...and it seems for nothing but a false sense of faith she had in her husband! But there's someone for everyone...I normally don't judge. I guess the ugliness on the inside shows through on the outside on some people. People can get what they deserve and Jared never, ever deserved my mother! I think Glenda and Jared are still married! Scary! They had kids! More scary! Jared and Glenda have grandkids...some girls...doesn't matter...but seriously scary!!! He is in his early sixties...but now there's Viagra! Fuck! Scariest thought of all!

...A pedophile on Viagra??? Yikes!

(And you may wonder why I have carried the burden of not knowing who else may have been affected by the wrath of Jared?!) I'm sick over it! I always have been.

When I finally told my mom and assured her she was fuckin' LUCKY to be rid of her husband, my sister was PISSED! My mom called Maureen and confronted her with my accusations. My sister reluctantly complied. She didn't say much of anything else. She just confirmed to my mom that he abused us. Then...Maureen had the fuckin' audacity to call *me* and bitch at me for telling our mother the truth! I told her I wanted to go to the police and turn his ass in. He deserved that at the very least...to go to jail for what he had done. She flat out told me "I won't do it! I won't say he did anything! I'll lie about it and I'll say you're lying! You won't get anywhere with it!" WOW! I couldn't believe what I was hearing! This was the day I had longed for almost *ALL MY FUCKIN" LIFE!* And Maureen had the fuckin' nerve to say she would deny *everything*?!? WTF?

I didn't understand until recently that Maureen at least had the decency to call and check on my mother after the devastating news was brought to light. Maureen did tell my mom that Jared said he would kill our mother if she had ever said anything. So why did Maureen demonstrate the inexplicably willing behavior all those years to comply with Jared's dirty deeds? Was Maureen mocking what *I* had told my mom about the threats or was that from her own true experience? Maureen would call my mom and check on her to be sure she was okay and Jared didn't kill her while she was sleeping. Whatever. My mother can handle herself. When she found out all this fucked up shit, she put that fuckin' 357 Magnum to his head and knew he wasn't worth ruining her life over too. I'm glad she didn't possibly have to go to prison for a douche bag. Being married to him was no picnic, I'm sure. And she found out. She found out what a man whore and sick bastard he really had been all along. And my sister, I don't know. I can't give her the benefit of the doubt these days…just like back then. She's all fucked up and I can't tell who is to blame.

*More on all that and why, along with lots of other relationships and the effects on them because of Jared in my next book…if y'all will have me.

CHAPTER **27**

So Many Women, Where in Hell Did He Find the Time?

So now my mother is getting divorced! This is by far the *best* thing that she could have *never* wanted!

My mother and I had finally established an open communicative relationship. I left school as a sophomore to come home. I knew my mom Mindy had lost a TON of weight. She was soooo tiny when I did finally see her! I truly almost didn't recognize her! She was sickly looking. She was so stressed from that fuckin' asshole and she had found out there were even more women than anyone can imagine. Women that Jared had made passes at, possibly assaulted, and maybe even raped. These women were wives of his cousins, wives of his close friends, and close friends of my mother's. None of them wanted to come forward at the time these events took place in fear of my mother's reaction and the affect it could possibly have on her health. Jared's own cousin, Mary Jane, had come forward three to four years prior accusing Jared of sexual misbehavior I was told. But people found it hard to believe and Jared convinced everyone that he could never do such a thing…she was his cousin! Sick fuckin' pervert. Poor Mary Jane. Putting herself in possible jeopardy of harm, and no one thought it was possible.

Now what?

CHAPTER **28**

Sick or Serial?

I LIKE TO watch present day shows like Criminal Minds, Law and Order/ Special Victims Unit, etc. I also became interested in, or intrigued is a better term, intrigued with the more twisted shows and movies such as the Saw Series of movies, Hostile, or Salem, the TV show in which I am currently enjoying. I watched anything discussing "bad" behavior or patterns in human behavior especially those that involved the abuse or torturing of others. I wanted to understand more of how these predators decided to do what they did to their victims. There has to be some reasons, right? I had some studies of psychology and philosophy classes in a few colleges, as well as viewing real life situations involving behaviors of "sick and twisted" people on talk shows and in the news. But that's about it. I wanted to understand what had happened to *me* and *why*.

The brazen move Jared had made in taking a photo of me naked and very obviously crying and reluctant to be in that situation baffled me for years! Why would he risk getting caught with it? It was child pornography, clear as day. What if my mother or one of my brothers found it by accident while cleaning or looking for something else? Don't you think that takes brass ones to have evidence that something obviously inappropriate was going on with a child??? He is a stupid fuck but surely he must have known he was breaking the law or he wouldn't have been so heavy on the threats. Jared's comment to me after it took a few minutes for that picture to develop was, "Now I can see how pretty you are any time I want." I slapped the color snapshot out of his hand that went from my head to my knees and exposing all in between. It fell to the ground. I was still without clothes and he and I both scrambled to get the photo off the floor. The stocky, shorter than I, son of a bitch got to it before I did! He yelled at me, "That's mine!" And he walked into his room and closed the door. I yelled "I fuckin' hate you!" No... "I love you daddy" was forced out of my mouth that time. I guess he was happy with his photo and that's all that mattered to him at the time.

Knowing a little more today about what some pedophiles do and how they may think...what drives them...I discovered why I think he took that one and only picture of me. (By the way, he never took a picture of me when I was fully clothed, ever that I can recall.)

According to behavioral scientists and criminal profilers that I have taken notice to on TV or in the news, these sick sons of bitches sometimes take pictures of their victims and treated these pictures as if they were *trophies*. And God and the world as my witness, I bet that sick fuck *STILL has my photo and more* of those he was able to isolate long enough to get into that position...naked! I hope and pray his current wife reads this or is told that this book is about *him*... and they go through *every inch of EVERYTHING he owns today*...and they will find such "trophies". I hope someone honest gets to them before he can destroy them. I truly believe something of that nature is there... among him...somewhere. Look through every magazine...I bet he still keeps some porn hidden under his bed, he kept stacks of the stag mags back in the day. Look in between the pages. Look in his garage...in cans...boxes...under shelves and drawers...leave no stone unturned. I'm sure there is a ton of shit! I find it difficult to believe he *"cured himself"* in any way. He is a sick man and did unforgivable things but never seemed to realize what he was doing was...considered wrong. I truly feel he thought in some fucked up way that he was "loving" children, or helping them *share* themselves and fulfill his own perverted urges…because he was and I strongly feel STILL MAY BE A PEDOPHILE! With that being said…he obviously wasn't *only* a pedophile because he had sought out more victims in grown, even pregnant women! So a pedophile *AND* a sex addict? Is he a serial offender of both? What the fuck *is* he???

CHAPTER **29**

Time to Pay the Piper

NO ONE CAN predict who may become a predator and seek out a child, possibly your child who may be grown and keeping a horrible secret themselves in fear of retaliation of Jared. I especially want then Pocono Mountain Department of Transportation for the school district to investigate and track down those special needs this predator drove to school and back...or God knows if he had stopped and did things to some before he took them home...I am pleading for the school to get in touch with these people and find out if he *affected* them as well. I called the school department in 2000 the moment I was told Jared had been working as a special needs children's bus driver...I flipped out! I made them aware of who he was, and that I was his former step daughter and made it VERY clear that he is to be NOWHERE around children! All they could tell me was that Jared no longer worked for them. They reassured me that they would note in his file that he was NEVER to be rehired again. I don't know what had transcribed to end his employment, but I sure would like to know! The thought makes me physically ill, but it's time to pay the piper and take some form of responsibility for the heinous behaviors.

I pray for those I imagine he has touched. I pray now that they find the strength and come forward and get this son of a bitch *away from anyone he could possibly ever hurt again!*

CHAPTER **30**

I Didn't Make *Justice* Part of my Pseudo Name for Nothing!

I need to make VERY clear what my intentions are with getting this book out there. The goal is to stop a man, a monster, an addict, a pedophile. Whatever the hell he is. If I was able to, I would have done so myself. I hope you understand now why I couldn't do a damn thing...until now. This is my way of seeking justice and closure for what was taken from me. My innocence, my sense of self worth, my reasons for living, and because I know he tragically has affected others...it burdens me even more to think he will always get away with his crimes. I need closure. I need to heal. I need to know I can go anywhere and Jared won't appear in the darkness, in a parking lot, anywhere. He doesn't deserve any mercy from me. I would never allow myself to feel pity for him. Writing this book has been the best therapy I could ask for.

I want him to pay for his horrific crimes the way others like him have, when caught. He needs to be caught! I need help from the media in spreading the word of a pedophile being possibly on the prowl in the Poconos! I need people to be smart, smarter than he is and talk! I need for those who figure out who his true identity is to talk to their families, their friends, everyone who has come in contact with this asshole that more than likely *still* terrorizes young children and grown women. Like I said...I doubt he woke up one day and said..."I don't think I'll have the urge to touch children anymore." We need to be realistic. I cannot legally do this by myself. My time has long expired. I am in search of those who still have the chance to put Jared where he belongs...behind bars. Behind bars for the rest of his life. Maybe then karma will kick in and he will meet a cell mate named Baby Cakes who likes little horny perverted men. It will then be left to fate. Maybe Jared will give himself up to the proper authorities and confess of his disgusting crimes of perversion.

I know Jared has enjoyed the kiss his freedom for far too long.

Now he can kiss my ass!

I told on you Jared...<u>I told big time!</u> You can't stay unknown forever.

I won't allow it.

It's your turn to be the scared little bitch!

You fuckin' owe honesty to me...to my family back then...to my family now...and to *all* your other victims...and their families...and now you owe it to your community as well, *Jared*.

As I am writing this last page, these last words, tears are falling down my face in relief.

I am now going to close my laptop and breathe the best I ever have in more than four decades.

I have done the right thing…my heart tells me so.

Mary J. Avalon

MaryJusticeAvalon@hotmail.com

Worth mentioning...

A very grateful thank you to Gina Girl who got me "over the hump" and let me know if I was any good at writing a book in the first place. She was the first person EVER to know any details of what I had gone through and I am thankful she gave me the courage to get over the fear of sharing it with others.

And there's Miss Dottie...A very special lady who turned her own personal tragedies into triumphs and still allow her to blossom. Dottie made me want to forge through the ugliness because she couldn't put my book down, even though I know it was painful for her as well. I am blessed to have crossed paths with her and call her my friend. She is a true inspiration!

Props out to my mother when I know her memories were churned up and spit out just to help me. She had been through enough herself and I appreciate her willingness to do the right thing as well. I love you mom.

And finally, I want to say I wish my sister well. You can't help those who don't wish to help themselves. I am wishing that *for* her. I have forgiven, but can I never forget. Things will never be as they should but I believe deep down there is goodness. Ignoring things doesn't make them disappear. I wish she would help herself, at least for those who love her.

"Tayla"...you will always be my "sista"! I love you girl!

You're an amazing miracle in all ways!

I finally want thank anyone who has taken the time to read my story. This part of my life wasn't pleasant by far, but if telling my story gives what happened to me anything positive...it is to have known I have had a purpose in life all along. If I can help just one other person find strength to speak out against abuse of <u>any</u> kind...It made all this sorrow and pain worth sharing. Sincerely,

M.J.A.

www.ingramcontent.com/pod-product-compliance
Lightning Source LLC
Chambersburg PA
CBHW022105160426
43198CB00008B/358